¡Burritos!

¡Burritos!

Hot on the Trail of the Little Burro

David Thomsen and Derek Wilson

GIBBS·SMITH
P
PUBLISHER

Salt Lake City

Published by
Gibbs Smith, Publisher
P.O. Box 667
Layton, Utah 84041
See our Web site: www.gibbs-smith.com

Design by David Charlsen, San Francisco, CA
Printed and bound in Korea

Library of Congress Cataloging-in-Publication Data
  Thomsen, David, 1971–
  Burritos: hot on the trail of the little burro / David Thomsen and Derek Wilson.
      p.   cm.
  ISBN 0-87905-835-8
  1. Burritos (Cookery) I. Wilson, Derek, 1965–. II. Title.
  TX836.T49 1998
  641.8-dc21   98-14033
                                                                 CIP

99 98   5 4 3 2 1

Contents

Our foods are prepared fresh throughout the day using Canola oil and other fine ingredients!!!

Introduction (ix)

Chapter 1 (1)

What Is a Burrito? More than the Sum of Its Parts

Chapter 2 (7)

History of the Burrito: Mystery, Intrigue, Romance, Beans

Chapter 3 (13)

Tortillas: The Edible Security Blanket

Chapter 4 (22)

Salsa: Spice for the Soul

Chapter 5 (37)

Beans and Rice: The Burrito's Rhythm Section

Chapter 6 (45)

Meat: The Carnivore's Candy

Chapter 7 (53)

Other Ingredients: Sometimes More Is Better

Chapter 8 (67)

How to Build and Eat the Perfect Burrito:
Instructions for People Who Never Read Instructions

Chapter 9 (75)

Burrito P.I.: How to Detect a Quality Taqueria

Chapter 10 (91)

The World's Best Burritos: The Joy of Not Cooking

Introduction

First of all, you should probably know that we have severe burrito addiction problems. If Betty Ford opened a burrito clinic, we wouldn't check in unless there was a decent taqueria nearby. We're convinced that a burrito craving is one of the most powerful forces on this planet. Those of you who have tasted true burrito perfection know what we're talking about. The burrito itch works its way into your brain unassumingly at first. You check your watch, grin to yourself, and briefly consider the plausibility of a burrito run. Feebly attempting to put your burrito fantasies on hold, you return to your activities. But before you can say Virgen de Guadalupe, mighty images of succulent overstuffed tortillas have completely taken over your consciousness. Relinquishing bodily control, you speed off to the taqueria faster than Scooby and Shaggy can put away a box of Scooby Snacks.

We didn't write this book on purpose. Honest. Like the discovery of penicillin, most of it happened accidentally. One day, while lunching at our favorite taqueria, we simultaneously stopped chewing and glanced down at the hefty bundles in our hands. As the bikini-clad Miller Beer Girl eyed us from the glossy poster on the wall, the idea for a book about burritos hit us like a mouthful of pickled jalapeños.

Armed with our incorrigible burrito appetites, a couple of notepads, a borrowed camera, and a pocketful of pesos, we set out on a journey in search of burrito perfection. Sometimes sampling six or seven burritos a day, we meandered from San Francisco down to Los Angeles, through the

Southwest, and into Mexico. With subsequent research trips the trail of the little burro stretched as far as the East Coast. We have probably put away more burritos than there would be unsold tickets for a Pat Boone concert at the Apollo Theater.

¡Burritos! Hot on the Trail of the Little Burro is the complete burrito resource. While it is not exclusively a cookbook, historical account, travel narrative, photographic essay, or sociology text, it contains elements of each—just like a burrito. It's bulging with kitchen secrets, burrito ingredient analyses, burrito philosophies, and burrito-lovers' resources, such as where to find the best

burritos available in the United States. Armed with this book, an adventurous spirit, and a sense of humor, you will have everything you need to reproduce or seek out the delectable flavors available at the world's top taquerias.

We'll admit that we take burritos seriously. Whenever we eat burritos together, conversation inevitably slips into discussions about tortilla texture, bean consistency, or ingredient distribution. But we hasten to acknowledge that, above all else, burritos are meant to be fun and frivolous. We hope you find this book to be the same.

Chapter 1
What Is a Burrito?
More than the Sum of Its Parts

If you don't have at least a vague sense of what a burrito is, chances are you've been living on a small farm in northern Mongolia for the past century. Saddle up the family yak and head for town because you've been missing out on one of the greatest human achievements since Stonehenge. Burritos are everywhere these days—upscale cafes, national chain restaurants, and neighborhood taquerias are all cashing in on burrito mania—but no two places make them in quite the same way. The definition of a burrito has broadened to include just about anything you can roll into a flour tortilla and eat with your hands.

So, just what *is* a burrito? Taken literally, the Spanish word *burrito* means little burro or little donkey. Over the years, the word became irreversibly linked to tortilla-rolled packages because they were also expected to carry a heavy load (which is good, because little donkeys are largely useless in the late-twentieth-century global economy). Generic burrito definitions can be found in many current English-language dictionaries. *The American Heritage Dictionary*, for example, defines burrito as "a flour tortilla wrapped around a filling, as beef, beans, or cheese." While this definition is starkly limiting, it manages to convey the general idea rather concisely.

The presence of the Spanish word *burrito* in the English dictionary highlights its ambiguous identity. Are burritos Mexican or American? Can they be both? The fact is, while the burrito's roots penetrate deeply beneath the Mexican desert, its subsequent maturation is firmly planted in the soil of America's multicultural garden. As we have adopted the Spanish word *burrito* into the English language, so has the cylindrical food pod it characterizes become fully integrated into the colorful international tapestry of American cuisine.

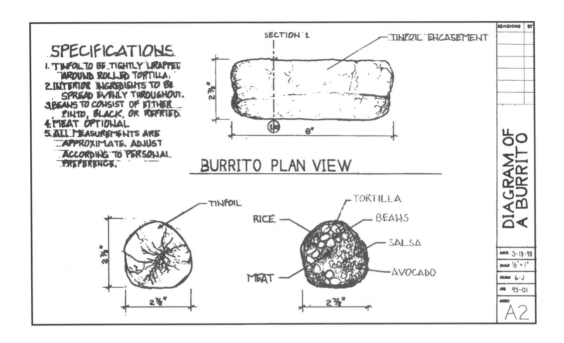

SPECIFICATIONS

1. TINFOIL TO BE TIGHTLY WRAPPED AROUND ROLLED TORTILLA.
2. INTERIOR INGREDIENTS TO BE SPREAD EVENLY THROUGHOUT.
3. BEANS TO CONSIST OF EITHER PINTO, BLACK, OR REFRIED.
4. MEAT OPTIONAL
5. ALL MEASUREMENTS ARE APPROXIMATE. ADJUST ACCORDING TO PERSONAL PREFERENCE.

SECTION 1

TINFOIL ENCASEMENT

8"

2⅞"

BURRITO PLAN VIEW

TINFOIL

RICE

MEAT

2⅞"

2⅞"

TORTILLA

BEANS

SALSA

AVOCADO

2⅞"

DIAGRAM OF A BURRITO

DATE 3-18-98
SCALE ½" = 1"
DRAWN 6-J
JOB 93-01
SHEET
A2

There is more to the meaning of the word *burrito* than a straightforward list of ingredients wrapped in a specific form of circular unleavened bread. With each and every burrito comes a certain significance. For many, burritos are merely an economical and convenient form of sustenance. For others, burritos serve as a respite from the dreary and hectic routine of modern life—comfort in a world of chaos. For still others, they are a fun and filling form of edible entertainment. For us, they are *the pinnacle of culinary creation.*

The following chart shows, according to our research, the prevailing burrito ingredients by region.

INGREDIENT	NORTHERN CA	SOUTHERN CA	SOUTHWEST	MIDWEST	EAST COAST	MEXICO	EUROPE
Mild Salsa			🌶	🌶	🌶		🌶
Hot Salsa	🌶	🌶	🌶			🌶	
Flour Tortilla	🌶	🌶	🌶	🌶	🌶	🌶	🌶
Guacamole		🌶				🌶	
Sour Cream				🌶	🌶		🌶
Refried Beans		🌶		🌶	🌶		
Pinto Beans	🌶						
Angry Cab Driver					🌶		
Black Beans			🌶				
Lettuce		🌶		🌶	🌶		🌶
Rice	🌶						
Cabbage						🌶	
Carne Asada	🌶					🌶	
Stewed Chicken	🌶						🌶
Machaca		🌶				🌶	
Carne Adobada			🌶				
BBQ Chicken			🌶		🌶		
Cilantro						🌶	

Descartes and Burritos

René Descartes (1596–1650), the founder of modern philosophy, is best known for his famous declaration, "I think, therefore I am." He argued that there are but two distinct independently existing substances in the world: the corporeal and the non-corporeal.

But how would Descartes' thinking have changed if he had lived in more burrito-friendly times? Undoubtedly, his statement about the certainty of existence would have been amended to "I eat burritos, therefore I am." His thoughts about mind and matter, about the distinct duality between consciousness and the material, would instead denote the absolute separation of all that is burrito and all that is not burrito. Descartes' realization that he could not doubt that he existed as a thinking substance, even though he could still doubt that he had a physical body, convinced him that mind could exist independently of matter. Which ultimately begs the question,

Can man exist without burritos?

The search for an adequate burrito definition may ultimately lack the comfort of certainty. Happily, burrito definitions are not universal, and burritos will always mean different things to different people. The security that comes through knowing absolutely is an illusion—a construct of our endless societal striving for unattainable perfection. So sit back and take the time to unquestioningly enjoy the pleasures of burrito consumption. Burritos *are* more than the sum of their parts, and burrito definitions are more than a specific combination of words. They are the combination of many peoples' *worlds*.

Chapter 2
History of the Burrito:
Mystery, Intrigue, Romance, Beans

The first time somebody handed me a burrito, man, I laughed.
What are you trying to feed me, a donkey?

—Jose Cuellar, Ph.D.
Chairman, Latino Studies Department
San Francisco State University

Although burritos have recently risen to near-staple status, surprisingly little is known about their origins. Many Americans incorrectly lump burritos into the same Mexican-food category that includes tacos, enchiladas, and quesadillas. In reality, as Professor Cuellar's quote suggests, many native Mexicans would give directions to the nearest barn if asked where to find a good burrito.

By the early 1800s, silver mines and cattle ranches were fairly well established in the Mexican states of Sonora and Chihuahua, which at the time stretched into areas now occupied by Arizona, New Mexico, and Texas. The American border was pushed south to its current location in the 1840s, establishing the Southwest as a region of ambiguous nationality and identity. As a result, the burrito, which developed in this area, has a nebulous nationality.

Primitive burritos were probably eaten soon after the development of the flour tortilla, but they did not earn their name or grow into their trademark bulging size until the mid-nineteenth century. The need for an easily transportable and economically feasible food arose as large numbers of Mexican miners, ranchers, and cowboys ventured north in search of shimmering fortunes during the California gold rush. Thanks to the established trade route along the Santa Fe Trail, wheat flour from the Midwest was readily available in the Southwest at the same time the tortilla-savvy immigrant population was flourishing. The creation of the first modern burrito probably occurred along this trail, somewhere in the dusty borderlands between Tucson and Los Angeles.

For almost a century, burritos remained a footnote in the complicated tale of Mexican-American relations and the mestizo cultures and cuisines that

BURRITO TIMELINE

10,000 B.C.
Agriculture begins. 11,850-year countdown to first burrito

6500 B.C.
Chile peppers cultivated in Latin America

5000 B.C.
Rice cultivation begins in Asia

4000 B.C.
Beer invented in ancient Mesopotamia, the first concrete step toward burrito production

3500 B.C.
First cultivation of beans

2000 B.C.
Greek experiments with democracy fail to prevent fights over the last chip

developed as a result. Although an awareness of Mexican cooking was spreading slowly in the United States, the majority of burritos were still consumed in Chicano communities, mining towns, and on the ranches that blanketed the southwestern United States and northern Mexico.

900 A.D.
Vikings get bored with reindeer jerky and ravage Northern Europe in search of more entertaining food

1000
Chinese invent gunpowder but remain stymied by tortillas

1400
Aztec Empire flourishing due to cultivation of early burrito components

1492
Colombus lands in the New World and discovers chile peppers

1506
Mona Lisa painted by Leonardo da Vinci. What's to smile about in a burritoless world?

1519
Hernán Cortés begins his conquest of Mexico and finds tortillas a staple in the native diet

Burritos began to make more regular urban appearances in the early 1960s. The first retail burritos in San Francisco were reputedly sold to a group of firemen at El Faro grocery store in 1961.* At the same time, landmark El Tepayac Cafe in Los Angeles was dishing up burritos to a multicultural and mostly blue-collar crowd. Pancho Rojas, whose grandfather founded the restaurant, recalls of the sixties, "There was a unity in our community, and people were enjoying burritos regardless of race."

By 1970, Mexican food (or at least what was being labeled and marketed as Mexican food) was being featured in mainstream American restaurants. With

---

* John Roemer, "The Cylindrical God," *San Francisco Weekly,* May 5, 1993.

1700	**1789**	**1798**	**1800**	**1850**	**1862**
Development of the flour tortilla	French Revolution — peasants tire of cake, demand burritos	Thomas Malthus concludes that humans are not capable of rolling burritos fast enough to keep up with demand	Relentless westward expansion of U.S. begins, fueling tension in the hemisphere but securing future Wal-Mart and Denny's sites	Invention of the modern burrito	Mexican army defeats the French in the battle of Puebla on Cinco de Mayo

the advent of the computer age and the continuing urban domination of the automobile, speed and convenience were becoming increasingly determinant factors in almost everything—even food selection. Suddenly the burrito began to get the nationwide attention it deserved.

With their combination of efficiency and Mexican flair, burritos exploded in the 1980s, leaving a permanent splatter of juicy bean residue on the psyche of the American consumer. Burritos are still riding this wave of popularity, and the recent wrap phenomenon that has made them even more palatable in conventional culinary circles will undoubtedly propel them into the next century as one of the defining elements of American cuisine.

1865
Tolstoy shelves idea for book about burritos and writes *War and Peace* instead

1898
Mariachi Vargas founded in Mexico

1916
Pancho Villa leads first attack on U.S. in over 100 years, proclaiming, "Give us back our burritos!"

1928
Postman Rudolph Hass cultivates the first Hass avocado tree

1931
The Rojas family, later to found El Tepayac Cafe, enters restaurant business in L.A.

1961
First retail burrito sold in San Francisco

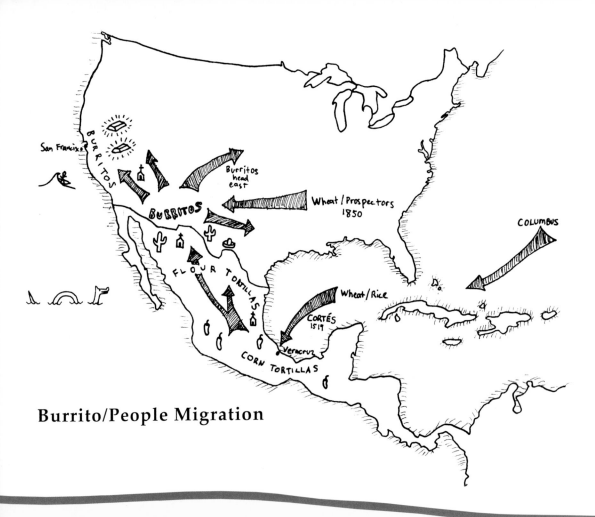

Burrito/People Migration

1985
Burrito begins to dominate the American culinary scene

1991
Los Gallos Taqueria founded by Miguel Jimenez

1997
World's largest burrito constructed in Mountain View, CA

2000
Burrito labeled by FDA as "world's most perfect food"

2001
Jimmy Carter holds Middle East Burrito party— eternal peace established

Chapter 3
Tortillas:
The Edible Security Blanket

Tortillas are the napkin, plate, fork and spoon of the Southwest.
—Butch Cassidy

Tortillas are the single most important and defining burrito ingredient. They give burritos both their physical and spiritual backbone, and it's easy to see that without them, burritos would not exist (no tortilla = no burrito). The crusty blandness of an inferior tortilla can imprison and nullify even the finest ingredients. In addition to providing secure protection for the burrito's succulent innards, tortillas supply the structural integrity and subtle flavors that round out the truly well-developed burrito.

Burrito Spanish, Lesson 1—Tortillas

English	Spanish	Pronunciation
tortilla	tortilla	tohr-TEE-yah
flour	harina	ah-REE-nah
corn	maiz	mah-EESS
salt	sal	sahl
Baywatch	Baywatch	BAY-watch

Tortillas have undoubtedly saved many cultures from the twin ravages of complicated silverware layouts and Wonder Bread. According to Mayan legend, the first corn tortillas were invented by a peasant for his hungry king around 10,000 B.C. Word of the easily prepared and nutritious discs made from ground dried corn kernels, salt, lime, and water spread quickly throughout Central and South America, where corn was a major crop. Many of the region's ancient civilizations were soon basing their diets around the simple unleavened bread, called *tlaxcalli* by the Aztec natives.

Flour Tortilla Press Line

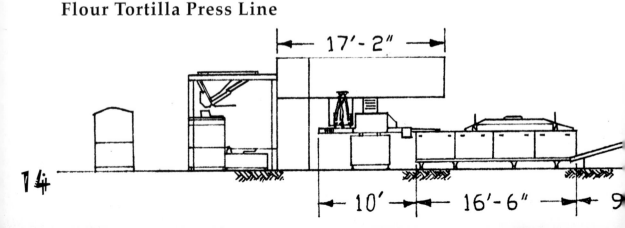

14

Flavored Tortillas

The advent of brightly colored flavored tortillas has pushed them into the realm of the gourmet. Many ridiculously expensive highbrow restaurants now feature flavored tortillas in main dishes. Manuel Berber, president of the Mi Rancho Tortilla Factory, explains, "They use them not only because they inject their entrees with color and flavor, but because they add an overall sense of fun."

Tortillas are now available in pesto, spinach, sun-dried tomato, wheat, onion and garlic, and tomato and basil. Mr. Berber is happy that the products are hot, but is quick to remind us that except for a small amount of flavoring, they are the same old tortilla that we have had for centuries.

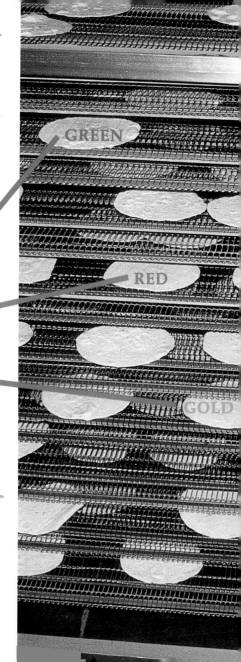

GREEN

RED

GOLD

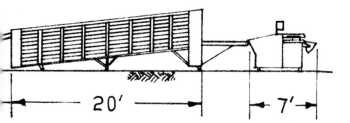

20'   7'

Soon after Hernán Cortés anchored his boat in Veracruz harbor in 1519 and began his conquest of the Aztec homeland, the Spaniards renamed the corn-based flat breads they found in use all over the region *tortillas*, which literally means smallish and flattened. Along with their relentless cultural domination, the Spaniards brought wheat to the New World, which they soon began to cultivate.

As the newly formed Latino culture spread north, establishing Christian missions along the way, it became apparent that the recently delivered wheat grew more easily than did corn in the arid climates of northern Mexico. Before long, people in this region were making tortillas using wheat flour. The greater strength of flour tortillas was the key to the development of the burrito. Perhaps owing to our "larger is better" cultural ethic, flour tortillas have become prevalent in the United States, while the smaller corn tortillas remain popular in most of Mexico.

A Visit to the Tortilla Factory

Remember watching *Willy Wonka and the Chocolate Factory* when you were a kid and thinking, "I'll never see a place as cool as that"? With one visit to a tortilla factory, you just may reconsider. Tortilla factories are a magical mixture of whirring Rube Goldberg machinery, energetic workers, and fresh aromas that could brighten even Edgar Allan Poe's darkest day—and the foreman may just be as wacky as Mr. Wonka himself. The pace is hectic, but all those warm tortillas keep the workers smiling like infomercial audience members.

The process is basically a large-scale version of home tortilla cookery. Flour is mixed with water, shortening, and salt in a huge noisy vat before giant wads of the rubbery dough are dumped into a peculiar machine that spits out perfectly rolled dough balls. The balls, called *bolitos*, are loaded onto a conveyor and flattened by a lightning-fast tortilla press, then fed into a multitiered oven. The baked tortillas pass through a cooling conveyor before they are counted and bagged.

Pay a visit to your local tortilleria in the early morning hours and you just might get a tour of the back room where you can watch miracles happen. Contact the Tortilla Industry Association (suggested company motto: Stop laughing— we're for real!) at (818) 981-2547 for directions to a manufacturing facility near you. You can also visit them on the web at www.tortilla-info.com.

Tortilla Recipes

It is possible to make perfectly round, thin tortillas at home. Theoretically, it is also possible to make a Buick Riviera at home, but your chance of success on the first try is about the same as with tortillas. Tortillas taste better and get better gas mileage, so forget the Buick for now.

In parts of rural northern Mexico and the Southwest, tortilla-making borders on an art form. Young girls serve apprenticeships with their mothers and grandmothers for years before they are able to effortlessly spin out paper-thin sheets of dough. So don't get discouraged if your first batch turns out misshapen and irregular.

During our Sonoran wanderings, we happened upon a roadside burrito stand where a woman out front was making flour tortillas by hand. After only one bite, we knew we had to find out how she made them. Shielding her squinting eyes from the burning sun, she graciously offered us the recipe below for

Sonoran tortillas. Where her recipe called for real lard, we have substituted vegetable shortening, which yields similar results. Although she was able to transform small balls of dough into perfect tortillas using only her hands and a rhythmic spinning motion, we recommend using a lightly floured rolling pin over a smooth flat surface (also floured).

Though all are delicious, the following tortilla recipes will give slightly different results. The Sonoran version will produce thin, dense tortillas, while the Fluffy version will yield tortillas that are slightly breadier. The Fluffy, Sundried Tomato, and Pesto recipes were developed with the help of Michael Tamayo from La Tortilla Factory in Santa Rosa, California.

Sonoran Tortillas

Yield: approximately 10 twelve-inch tortillas

Ingredients

4 cups unbleached flour
1½ teaspoons salt
4 tablespoons vegetable shortening

1¾ cups warm water (not hot)
Extra flour

Equipment

Rolling pin
Large flat surface
Extra flour
Towel (large enough to cover bowl)
Large griddle or frying pan

Large mixing bowl
Fork
Knife
Wooden spatula or spoon

Fluffy Tortillas

Yield: approximately 10 twelve-inch tortillas

Ingredients

4 cups unbleached flour
1½ teaspoons salt
1½ teaspoons baking powder

3 tablespoons vegetable shortening
1½ cups warm water

Tortilla Instructions:

Combine the dry ingredients in a large bowl. Add the vegetable shortening and warm water and continue mixing. Once the dough shows some cohesiveness, knead it on a floured surface for a few minutes until it becomes uniform. If the dough is still sticking to your hands, add a bit more flour. Conversely, if it is too stiff and unmanageable, add a bit more water. The larger your intended tortillas, the more water you should use.

Now separate the dough into bolitos (little balls). Pull off enough dough to form a two-inch-diameter ball and roll it between your palms until it is round. Put the finished bolitos on a tray, cover, and let them rest for 20–25 minutes.

Place a bolito on a floured surface and roll with a rolling pin into the thinnest possible circle. After several passes the dough will begin to hold its shape. Be patient. It is very difficult to create a round tortilla, so we recommend taking the easy way out—use a knife and simply cut a circle out of your amoeba-like flattened dough.

Using a wooden spatula for assistance, carefully place the uncooked tortilla onto a hot griddle or large frying pan on high heat for about thirty seconds on each side, or until light brown spots appear. With a good attitude and a little practice, you'll be well on your way to getting rid of napkins, plates, forks and spoons forever.

Note to the Health Conscious

It is possible to make tortillas with little or no shortening. Texture, resiliency, and flavor may suffer slightly, but they will still be pretty darned tasty. Try experimenting with about 2 tablespoons of shortening instead of five, or eliminate it altogether.

Sundried Tomato Tortillas

Yield: approximately 10 twelve-inch tortillas

Ingredients

Sonoma Dried Tomatoes (follow instructions on label for presoaking)
1 additional tablespoon water
1 recipe Fluffy Tortillas

To the recipe for Fluffy Tortillas, add 4 tablespoons of sundried tomatoes and 1 additional tablespoon of warm water, and follow tortilla instructions.

Pesto Tortillas

Yield: approximately 10 twelve-inch tortillas

Ingredients for Pesto

1 large bunch basil, stemmed
  and chopped
1/8 cup olive oil
1/3 cup pine nuts
3 cloves garlic

1 teaspoon salt
Dash of pepper
Water as needed for blending
  (less than 1/4 cup)

Pesto Instructions:

Blend nuts and garlic until finely chopped. Slowly blend in olive oil and basil, adding water as needed. To Fluffy Tortillas recipe, add 4 tablespoons pesto and follow tortilla instructions.

Chapter 4
Salsa: Spice for the Soul

Contrary to popular belief, Mexican food is not hot, which is why salsas were created.

—Jose Antonio Burciaga, Chicano activist,
poet, muralist, and author,
in *Drink Cultura*

The Mythical Origins of Salsa

One evening while preparing the usual feast of tortillas, beans and meat stew for her family, Maria Espinoza de la Mortadella heard a faint whisper blow through her dilapidated wooden doorway, linger around the glowing coals in her fire pit, and fade away. Though startled at first, the soothing, otherworldly quality of this voice did not scare her, but instead sparked a certain curiosity deep within her soul. Maria was not a fragile woman, and the wrinkles that fractured her leathery brown face when she smiled spoke of wisdom rather than age. Without thinking, she stopped stirring the aromatic mixture that bubbled in front of her and shuffled toward the starlit blackness that lurked just outside her door. Becoming aware of the rhythmic pounding of her heart, she grasped the splintery door frame and peered around the corner. No one was there. But before she could resume her preparations, it came again.

"Salsa," it coaxed. "Salsa fresca . . ."

Though the people of her village tried for many years to persuade Maria to tell them what happened next, she resolutely refused. When they asked her how she had learned to make the delicious and colorful mixture she had taught them to call *salsa*, Maria would simply tilt her head slightly toward the endless blue sky, slide her deep brown eyes up in their sockets, and grin mischievously.

Burritos and Salsa

A burrito without salsa is like a burger without ketchup—
*while it is still edible and maybe even tasty, **it's just not the same, man.***

—Jim Morrison

Despite the ketchup analogy, salsa is definitely more than a mere condiment. Salsa is a vital burrito component that serves to complement the other more-massive burrito ingredients. Like John Belushi at a debutante ball, salsa intensifies and enlivens burrito flavors. Additionally, its bright colors and crunchy textures are visually and physically pleasing. Good salsa can border on the spiritual and, when coupled with burritos, can propel the consumer into heavenly bliss.

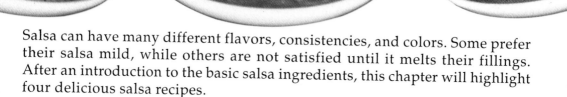

Salsa can have many different flavors, consistencies, and colors. Some prefer their salsa mild, while others are not satisfied until it melts their fillings. After an introduction to the basic salsa ingredients, this chapter will highlight four delicious salsa recipes.

Burrito Spanish, Lesson 2—Salsa

English	Spanish	Pronunciation
tomato	tomate	toh-MAH-teh
onion	cebolla	seh-BOH-yah
coriander	cilantro	see-LAHN-troh
garlic	ajo	AH-ho
avocado	aguacate	ah-gwah-KAH-teh
salsa	salsa	SAHL-sah
My mouth is burning	La boca esta en fuego	lah BOH-kah es-TAH en FWEH-goh

Salsa Ingredients

While entire books have been written about salsa, there are several requisite ingredients that warrant special attention. The majority of these are now available in large supermarkets, but if you are having trouble, check smaller markets in Latino neighborhoods. If you are desperate, there are several suppliers who you can contact over the World Wide Web. For peppers try www.emall.com; for avocados, www.rgv.net; for herbs such as cilantro and cumin, www.pureandnaturalspices.com. The Mexico Corporation, in Burbank, California, at (818) 372-6719, is an excellent source for herbs, spices, and dried chiles, and will ship COD.

Chile Peppers—the heart of the heat

No other single food item has enjoyed quite the same level of adoration, scrutiny, and appreciation as the chile pepper. Known scientifically as capsicums, chiles have inspired international festivals, volumes of books, heated debates, and entire national cuisines. Without peppers, we would truly be living in a greatly diminished culinary landscape.

Though he is inexplicably more recognized for other less-important achievements, Christopher Columbus introduced peppers to Europe, where they eventually spread and became a regular part of the cuisines of such faraway places as India, southwestern China, the Middle East, and Africa. The pepper's burning properties were clearly designed by nature to protect it, and with the exception of certain species of birds, humans are the only animals known to ingest the fruits on purpose.

So why do we love the food that burns us so? The strange and incomprehensible human disposition would probably be a sufficient explanation, but there are some practical reasons. Chiles contain higher concentrations of vitamin A than any other plant and twice as much vitamin C as oranges. Peppers act as a digestive aid by stimulating gastric secretions and increase the metabolic rate. Chiles are also rumored to be an aphrodisiac. While the heat produced through the ingestion of capsicums can be initially unpleasant, the burning provokes the release of endorphins in the brain that cause feelings of mild euphoria and satisfaction.

The Original Pepper Spray

The uses of chile peppers are not all positive. According to legend, the Incas created a wall of toxic smoke between themselves and the invading Spaniards by burning giant piles of hot peppers. The fumes contained natural irritants that temporarily blinded the conquerors.

There are an overwhelming variety of chile peppers in existence, but only a few are readily available in American stores. Other than the bland bell, the jalapeño is the most recognized chile in the United States. It is also the pepper most readily associated with burritos and Mexican cooking. While quite hot for most of us, jalapeños fall in the middle of the pepper heat scale. When dried, jalapeños are called *chipotles*.

Serrano peppers are smaller than jalapeños, but they pack more punch than the giant Kool-Aid guy. In northern Mexico, the serrano is the chile of choice, but be careful when you cook with it: its potency can be overpowering.

Jalapeño

To really explore the outer boundaries of earthly spiciness (and masochism), sample a habañero pepper. *Avoid handling habañeros at all costs, especially if you wear contact lenses;* a microdrop in the eye can be devastating. Habañeros are a definite case of evolutionary overkill, similar to when you accidentally hit your shin on the coffee table: it doesn't need to be nearly that painful to convince you not to do it again.

Other peppers that are used in burrito cooking include pasillas, chiles de arbol, New Mexican chiles, and Californian chiles.

Cilantro—love it or leave it

There is no in-between with cilantro; people either love it or hate it. Known as *coriander* or *Chinese parsley* in many parts of the United States, this aromatic herb is cultivated and eaten throughout Mexico. Its unmistakable flavor adds both kick and color to salsa. Cilantro is sold in most major supermarkets, but if it is not available in your area, it can be easily grown at home or stolen from the neighbor's window box.

Onions—it's okay to cry

You know what these are. If you don't, maybe you're reading the wrong book. Try some John Grisham.

Tomatoes—the ubiquitous fruit

Although almost any tomato will produce great salsa, Roma tomatoes, with their bright red hue and sturdy structure, are preferred. While we're on the subject, let's put an old controversy to rest: a fruit is defined as the mature ovary of an angiosperm. It sounds really sexy and all, but what this definition means is that a fruit is something that grows out of a flower. Tomatoes grow from the flowers of the tomato vine, so once and for all: the tomato is a fruit.

Tomatillos—so many names, so little recognition

These tiny balls of tartness are not related to tomatoes at all but rather the cape gooseberry. About the size of golf balls, their wrinkled husks should always be removed before use. They turn yellow when ripe but are usually used in their unripe green state. If tomatillos are not available fresh in your local market, you can order them canned through the mail from Melissa's World Variety Produce at (800) 468-7111. Tomatillos are also called *tomate verde*, *miltomate*, *tomate de hoja*, or *fresadilla*.

Serrano

27

Authors' tip

Never crush dried hot peppers in your friend's coffee grinder.
Most people don't want spicy coffee in the early morning. In fact,
they can get downright hostile about it and usually don't care
much if your salsa turned out brilliantly.

Living in FEAR of Spice

There's nothing worse than a gloating hot-pepper snob—but, then again, a pep-
perless burrito might as well be a bagel dog. To curb your overwhelming
shame, those of you who live in fear of spicy foods might consider a training
regimen. Boost your confidence with a week of bell peppers before you move
on to something a little more powerful, like poblano or pasilla peppers. Slowly
increase the quantity and pungency of your pepper intake until you can
munch down handfuls of serrano peppers while your stunned friends look on
in awe. If the fire burning inside your mouth gets too hot, try chewing on a spoonful of peanut butter, drinking a glass of milk, or eating some yogurt rather than
slugging down a gallon of water. While cold water may provide temporary relief,
peanut oils and lipoproteins found in milk and yogurt will actually dilute the
pepper's heat-inducing oils.

**Cross Section
of a Pepper**

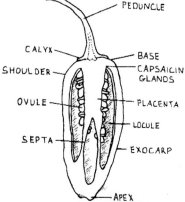

Salsa Recipes

Good salsa is not difficult to make—in fact, with fresh ingredients, it is virtually impossible to make bad salsa. We like to say, "You can only mess up this stuff at the store." Truly superior salsa relies upon subtleties that are only discernible with practice and determination. Because we know you would never bother to do it yourself, we have sorted through countless ingredient combinations and quantities and spoken with expert salsa chefs to make the following four recipes available to you. We can state with the utmost confidence that they are the absolute best salsa recipes you will find. Batteries not included. See contest rules for details.

Salsa Fresca

Long a staple in Mexico (no table setting is complete without a bowl of it), salsa fresca is also the most widely used in American burrito shops. It is not complicated, but there's little doubt that when these five ingredients are mixed together, magic happens. This particular recipe was revealed to us by Luis Antonio and Carlos at a tiny taqueria in Pitiquito, Mexico, where they call it *bandera salsa* after the white, green, and red colors of the Mexican flag. It is also called *pico de gallo*, *salsa Mexicana*, *salsa ranchera*, *salsa cruda*, or *picadillo*.

Ingredients

½ white onion, finely diced
4 Roma tomatoes, finely diced
¼–½ cup cilantro, chopped
1 teaspoon salt (or to taste)

1 jalapeño, finely diced
1 teaspoon garlic powder or 2 cloves garlic, diced (optional)
Juice from ¼ lime (optional)

Equipment

1 sharp knife for dicing and slicing
1 stirring spoon

1 medium-sized bowl
Large cutting surface

Dump everything into a bowl and mix until the ingredients are evenly distributed. For a more complicated and equally delicious flavor, include crushed garlic and lime juice. This recipe makes roughly 2 cups and keeps for about one week when covered and refrigerated.

Salsa Verde

This delicious recipe is a slight variation on the green salsa available at El Farolito Taqueria in San Francisco, California (see chapter 10 for review). While theirs is as hot as a summer day in Sonora, we have suggested a smaller quantity of serranos. In Mexico, this type of salsa is sometimes called *guacamole*, but we aren't in Mexico, so forget about it. Amaze your friends!

Ingredients

1 Hass avocado, peeled and sliced
12 tomatillos, husked and finely diced
3–4 serrano chiles, finely diced
2 teaspoons oregano, freshly diced

Dash of ground cumin
4 garlic cloves, crushed and diced
½ teaspoon salt

Equipment

1 large sharp knife for dicing
  and chopping
1 medium-sized bowl

1 fork for mixing
Large cutting surface

Using a fork, mash and stir the avocado, tomatillos, serranos, and garlic in a medium-sized bowl for several minutes, adding the salt, cumin, and oregano as the mixture becomes uniformly creamy. Alternatively, you can use a blender, but the result will not be as creamy. Serve with corn chips, tortillas, or burritos. This recipe makes about 2½ cups and will keep for a few days in the refrigerator.

31

Capsaicin

H₃CO, HO— (benzene ring) —C—N—C—(CH₂)₆—C—CH₃ with CH₃, H₂, H, O

$$H_3CO-, HO-\bigcirc-\underset{H_2}{C}-\underset{H}{N}-\overset{O}{\underset{\|}{C}}-(CH_2)_6-\underset{CH_3}{\overset{CH_3}{\underset{|}{C}}}-CH_3$$

Measuring the Burn

Capsaicin, an amide-type alkaloid, is the match that lights the fire in your mouth when you eat peppers. A subjective taste test developed in 1912, called the Scoville Organoleptic Test, established the Scoville unit as the measure of a pepper's hotness. Who knows what this means exactly, but Organoleptic sure sounds interesting. Today, high-pressure-liquid chromatography (the greatest of all the chromographs) is the preferred method for quantifying capsaicinoids in capsicums. Habañero peppers weigh in at a crushing 325,000 Scoville units maximum, while jalapeños top out at 5,000. In between are serranos, with a maximum of 23,000. Because the pungency of the same type of pepper can vary greatly with differing soils, climates, and seasons, both measurements should only be used as a general guide. You're better off sampling a particular pepper for yourself and adjusting the quantities you use in your cooking accordingly.

Dihydrocapsaicin

$$H_3CO-, HO-\bigcirc-\underset{H_2}{C}-\underset{H}{N}-\overset{O}{\underset{\|}{C}}-(CH_2)_4-\underset{H}{\overset{}{C}}=\underset{H}{\overset{}{C}}-\underset{H}{\overset{CH_3}{\underset{|}{C}}}-CH_3$$

Blendy Salsa

If you need fresh salsa quick, this is your bag, baby.

Ingredients

2 large tomatoes
  or 4 Roma tomatoes, diced
1–2 serrano chiles, stemmed

1 teaspoon salt
2 cloves garlic, skins removed

Equipment

Blender

Put everything in the blender and whirl away. Blend only in quick pulses, otherwise air gets whipped into the salsa and changes the consistency.

Salsa Roja

This delicious salsa has a unique smoky taste and a rich maroon color (despite its name). It gives burritos a fiery kick and can also be enjoyed with chips. This recipe was graciously given to us by Los Gallos Taqueria in Redwood City, California, and is absolutely the best of its kind.

Ingredients

Roughly 50 dried chiles
de arbol, stemmed
3 cloves garlic, diced
½ onion, diced
4–6 tomatillos, husked
½ teaspoon pepper

1 teaspoon oregano,
dried or freshly diced
2 teaspoons salt
⅓–½ cup corn or olive oil
Water as needed

Equipment

Blender
Small frying pan

Small pot

Cook the chiles de arbol in oil over medium heat until about half are blackened. Boil the tomatillos in water until they become soft (roughly 10 minutes). Blend the onion, garlic, tomatillos, and chiles (with the oil) until smooth, adding a bit of water as necessary. Add the salt, pepper, and oregano, and blend for a few more seconds. This recipe makes roughly 2 cups and keeps for two weeks in the refrigerator.

Store-bought Salsa—when desperation calls

Any bottled salsa will never be on par with fresh homemade mixtures. There are always situations, however, when whipping up a fresh batch is not possible. A few nationally available bottled salsas are mildly tolerable, though their uniformly mediocre quality is baffling. We painfully sampled fifteen jars of medium spicy chunky-style mixtures in vacuum-sealed jars. This list highlights some of the best and worst.

La Victoria. If we had to choose a favorite, this would be it. Uncharacteristically un-ketchupy, though very salty.

Safeway Southwest Salsa. More complicated sweet and mild flavor than others with a nearly recognizable texture.

Pace Thick and Chunky. Lumpy and spicy, but ketchupy and too sweet.

Ortega Thick and Chunky. Tasteless pasta sauce mixed from canned tomato remnants.

Granny Goose. The worst of the lot. Thick and syrupy, with a bitter, spoiled aftertaste. You're better off with a bottle of Heinz.

Your supermarket might carry some locally produced salsas. They are often elusively stored in random locations around the store, and are usually fresher than the national brands. If you have a choice, get the hot version—chiles were nearly nonexistent in the medium versions we tested.

Bottled salsa is also available in staggering quantities on the World Wide Web. Try www.salsacentral.com, or www.offthedeepend.com.

Burrito Haiku

Meal so cheap
Swinging piñata
I love you

Magical smells
Remove crumpled tinfoil
I am happy

Cylindrical
Bundle of joy
Feeling full

Rolled with love
Anticipation unbearable
Smiling juicy bite

Chapter 5
Beans and Rice:
The Burrito's Rhythm Section

The rhythm section of a musical group provides the foundation on which the rest of the music is free to build. Often predictable but always necessary, the drums and bass are the syncopated workhorse that keeps the musical flow cohesive. Beans and rice do the same for a burrito.

In addition to keeping a large portion of the world's population alive and smiling, beans and rice form the filling and flavorful cornerstone around which the other burrito ingredients can be arranged. Sadly, some taquerias skimp on the quality of their beans and rice. Neglected beans deteriorate into crusty kibble nuggets, and rice dries into starchy wood chips. The best burritos are made by people who know that every ingredient, down to each individual bean and each grain of rice, is important. Poor bean and rice quality reveals a lack of passion and an impaired burrito consciousness, like a would-be green thumb calling the one tomato plant in his backyard a garden.

Beans

The first half of the burrito's rhythm section is composed of the mighty bean, one of the foodstuffs introduced to the Old World by the New. The importance of beans, especially to the Mexican culinary tradition, cannot be overstated. There are many types of beans, but pinto and black are the most common in burrito cookery. Refried beans, that other famous burrito ingredient, are made from pintos.

Bean cultivation, although ancient, is young compared to many other crops. Beans do not make an appearance in the historical record until approximately 3500 B.C., almost three millennia after the first cultivation of the chile pepper. By the time the Spanish discovered beans in the sixteenth century, frijoles had already become a vital component of the indigenous diet. Their high protein content and versatility made them a perfect complement to other staple crops of the region, such as corn. Beans also contain large quantities of calcium, phosphorus, and iron.

Burrito Spanish, Lesson 3—Beans and Rice

English	Spanish	Pronunciation
beans	frijoles	free-HOH-lehs
black	negro	NEH-groh
refried	refrito	reh-FREE-toh
rice	arroz	ah-RROS

Pinto and **Black** Beans

Pinto beans are perfectly suited to hot dry climates and require limited labor to achieve good yields. Named for the reddish brown splotches that streak their pale skins (*pinto* means spotted), these delightfully hearty little protein capsules give the burrito a solid heft and bulk that makes polishing one off a genuine accomplishment. Black beans are prevalent in southern Mexico but are preferred by many in burritos. Smaller than pintos, with slightly tougher skins, cooked black beans retain their individual integrity more than pintos.

Bean Recipes

Bean recipes don't vary a great deal, so once you are familiar with their basic ingredients, it is easy to experiment. Impatience is the bean's one true enemy, and successful preparation hinges on long slow cooking. The following recipe can be used for both regular pintos and black beans.

Ingredients

2½ cups pinto or black beans
10 cups water
3 ounces salt pork or 3 tablespoons
    shortening (optional)
1 tablespoon salt

¼ cup fresh oregano
Pinch cumin
½ teaspoon black pepper
3 garlic cloves, chopped

Equipment

5-quart pan or Crock-Pot

Chopping knife

If you are using salt pork, melt it in the pan first. Otherwise, throw all of the ingredients except salt into the pan and bring to a boil. Reduce heat to simmer. Now for the tough part—cover and wait for three hours. You can peek if you like but it will still take three hours. After three hours, add the salt and simmer for 20 to 30 minutes more. Turn off the heat and wait as long as you can, perhaps until the following night. The flavor supposedly ages nicely if you do this, but nobody really knows because everyone digs in right away.

Refried Beans

Refried beans are pintos that have been cooked, left behind the barn for a few days, then mashed with a little lard into a smooth paste and reheated. The result is a rich smoky concoction that gives burritos a malleable denseness that many people find irresistible. It is also possible to re-fry black beans, but they are decidedly less tasty when prepared this way. Refried beans are widely available canned, but so is dog food; you're much better off with the homemade stuff.

Ingredients

3 cups of cooked pinto beans
   from the above recipe
2 tablespoons shortening
½ onion, finely chopped

½ teaspoon salt
Dash black pepper
2 cloves garlic, chopped
Pinch cumin

Equipment

Frying pan
Pot or large bowl

Chopping knife

Using a large spoon, mash the cooked beans in a pot or large bowl. Melt the shortening in a large frying pan, then add everything but the beans. Get it good and hot, and then add the beans. Stir constantly and continue mashing until their consistency is to your liking. Enjoy!

Suggested Reading

John Steinbeck's *Tortilla Flat*, published in 1935, tells how beans wrapped in a tortilla keep the Cortez family in good health and good spirits. The following excerpt reveals that Steinbeck was in many ways a visionary.

The visiting nurse, trained in child psychology, said kindly, Freddy, do you get enough to eat?

Sure, said Alfredo.

Well, now. Tell me what you have for breakfast.

Tortillas and beans, said Alfredo.

The nurse nodded her head dismally to the principal. What do you have when you go home for lunch?

I don't go home.

Don't you eat at noon?

Sure. I bring some beans wrapped up in a tortilla.

Actual alarm showed up in the nurse's eyes, but she controlled herself.

At night what do you have to eat?

Tortillas and beans.

Her psychology deserted her. Do you mean to stand there and tell me you eat nothing but tortillas and beans?

Alfredo was astonished. Jesus Christ, he said, what more do you want?

Rice

Archeological excavations have uncovered sealed pots of rice in China that are nearly 8,000 years old, but the historical record of active cultivation dates to about 5000 B.C. Rice was brought to the New World by the Spanish, who had been introduced to it by the Arabs. Though it is considered an essential component at meals all over the world, particularly in Asia, it is one of the most overlooked grains in the United States. In many cultures, rice is considered fast food. Its labor-intensive reputation in this country probably says something about the pace of our lives.

At least 30 percent of the world's population subsists almost exclusively on rice and rice-based products. China alone consumes enough rice in one day to fill 5.4 billion burritos. Rice is high in protein, completely fat-free, and full of energy-producing carbohydrates. **Plus, it's cheap**. So stop looking at rice as that big bag of stuff in the back of the cupboard that takes too long to cook, and start being impressed.

Rice Recipe

Part of the beauty of rice, aside from its pure white color and elegant petite shape, is the fact that it is relatively easy to cook. Short of spilling hot water on the cat, there isn't much that can go wrong. Follow this simple recipe and your reward will be top-quality burrito rice. According to Mexican folklore, if you cook rice while frowning, your dreams will be periodically haunted by images of Richard Simmons doing the macarena while dressed as a Keebler elf. So smile—rice is fun!

Ingredients

1¾ cups white rice
1 tablespoon olive or vegetable oil
2 cups water
1 cup chicken broth

½ yellow onion, diced
2 small/medium tomatoes, diced
3 cloves garlic, diced
1½ teaspoon salt

Equipment

2-quart saucepan and lid
Chopping knife

Blender
Golden Retriever (optional)

Puree the tomato, onion, and garlic, and set aside. Fry the raw rice in the oil over medium heat, stirring constantly until it begins to turn golden brown—about 7 to 10 minutes. Add the tomato/onion/garlic mixture and cook until most of the moisture has been absorbed, stirring if needed. Add the broth, water, and salt, and bring to a boil, stirring occasionally. Do not cover. Reduce heat to simmer, then play with the Retriever for about 15 minutes. When all the liquid is absorbed, cover and let sit for 10 minutes before serving. This recipe makes about 7 cups of rice.

Chapter 6
Meat: The Carnivore's Candy

We stepped into the grocery store, ducking under the piñatas that hung from the ceiling, and quickly gathered that it was similar to many of the other Mexican markets in small-town central California. The neatly stacked rows of imported hot sauces, spices, and canned goods fronted a small lunch area that served as much local news as food. As we approached the deli counter, trying to decide what type of burrito to order, we suddenly noticed an enormous cow head, replete with a hanging tongue and intact eyeballs, sitting on a table next to the sink in back. While everyone else in the market went about their business, even sipping tripe soup in a chair *right next to the head*, as hard as we tried, we could not help but stare at the massive skinned mound of flesh and bones.

While Mexicans are more comfortable with their carnivorous nature, American culture has placed a stigma on eating certain parts of animals, let alone watching them be cut up and prepared. As long as there is a disconnect between the hunk of cooked flesh we are eating and the dead animal it came from, meat seems to be more palatable to Americans. Our culture is packaged and we like our meat that way too. When we sampled a tongue  burrito, even though the meat was tender and tasty, it was admittedly hard to get past the fact that it was, after all, *a cow's tongue*. While it may take guts to eat guts, these items make the menu at a taqueria a little more exciting.

Meat is one of the more difficult burrito ingredients to prepare, but its true success hinges on a flavorful integration with the beans, rice, and salsa. Many taquerias, concentrating almost exclusively on providing top-quality meat, let the caliber of the other ingredients slip into mediocrity. As with a fulfilling, multidimensional life, a little balance is the key.

Top Five Coolest Mexican State Names

Michoacan

Zacatecas

Oaxaca

Chihuahua

Quintana Roo

Owing to the Mexican culinary tradition, the types of meats available in burritos are as varied as the styles in which they are prepared. Taquerias roast, grill, and boil chicken for burrito usage. Pork is marinated and spit-roasted, fried, made into sausage, or cured and grilled. Beef is seasoned and grilled, marinated and stewed or dried and shredded. Beef brains, tongue, intestines, and head meat are also cooked and served in burritos at authentic taquerias.

Burrito Spanish, Lesson 4—Meat

English	Spanish	Pronunciation
meat	carne	KAHR-neh
chicken	pollo	POH-yoh
grilled beef steak	carne asada	KAHR-neh ah-SAH-dah
shredded beef	machaca	mah-CHAH-kah
beef brains	sesos	SEH-sohs
beef head meat	cabeza	kah-BEH-suh
beef tongue	lengua	LEN-gwah
vegetarian	vegitariano	veh-jee-tah-ree-AH-no
intestines	tripitas	tree-PEE-tahs
pork sausage	chorizo	choh-REE-soh
marinated pork	al pastor	al pas-TOHR
fried pork	carnitas	kahr-NEE-tahs

Meat Recipes

We have selected our favorite burrito meat recipes for your enjoyment—one *al pastor*, two *carne asada*, and one *pollo*. The cut of the meat you select can have a huge effect on the quality of your final product, as well as on the size of your grocery bill, so we have tried to specify what to buy.

Al Pastor

Al pastor, meaning literally shepherd style, is a traditional way to prepare pork, lamb, and goat meat that originated in northern Mexico. Historically, pigs and goats were slow-roasted whole over a mesquite fire, but over time, preparation methods evolved. Similar to the roast lamb from Greek delis, taquerias stack the marinated pork al pastor into a large cylindrical heap and cook it on a vertical spit. Juicy chunks are sliced off as the outer layers become cooked. The highly seasoned, succulent slices make for a truly decadent burrito experience.

Ingredients

½ pound pork leg (boneless)
4 dried California or
  New Mexico chiles, stemmed
2 dried pasilla chiles, stemmed
2 cloves
½ teaspoon cumin

½ teaspoon pepper
¾ cup white vinegar
¾ cup water
1 teaspoon salt
½ head of garlic, peeled
2 tablespoons corn or olive oil

Equipment

Blender
Medium frying pan

Bowl with cover

Cook the chiles in the vinegar, water, cumin, pepper, salt, and cloves over medium heat until they become very soft. Pour the whole mixture (be careful or be burned) into the blender, add the garlic, and puree. Heat the oil, add the blended mixture, and simmer for fifteen minutes. Cut the pork into small chunks, put into a bowl, pour the marinade over the top, and let it sit covered overnight in the refrigerator. Slowly grill the marinated meat in a splash of oil over low heat (be patient) and enjoy in a burrito.

Al Pastor

Carne asada, literally grilled or roasted meat, is very common on both sides of the border. The two recipes presented below are fairly standard but were developed with the help of Taqueria El Menudo and the staff at 7 Mares restaurant in Redwood City, California. The second recipe is quick and not quite as savory as recipe one, but the results are nonetheless delectable.

Marinated Carne Asada

Ingredients

½ pound beef (top loin, flap meat, tenderloin, NY strip, or top sirloin steak, trimmed of fat)
1 teaspoon olive or vegetable oil

Marinade

¼ teaspoon cumin (comino)
1 tablespoon oregano, finely diced
2 cloves garlic, diced

1½ teaspoon lime juice
 (about ½ a lime)
1 teaspoon salt
¼ cup beer

Equipment

1 medium-sized bowl for marinating
1 very sharp carving knife

1 refrigerator
1 large griddle or frying pan

Combine the garlic with cumin, oregano, lime juice, salt, and beer. Drink the rest of the beer; it will make you feel better. Slice the meat into very small cubes (less than a half-inch thick), put them in the marinade, cover and refrigerate. After a good night's rest, retrieve the meat from the refrigerator and take a minute to notice how good it smells. Heat the oil in a frying pan and grill the marinated meat until toasty brown marks appear. Add a dash of salt, a splash of beer, and some of the marinade to the meat while it is cooking. This recipe makes enough carne asada for three burritos.

Quick Carne Asada

Ingredients

½ pound beef (flap meat is best, but tenderloin, NY strip, or top sirloin
 steak are all sufficient)

Pinch cumin (comino) 1 teaspoon olive oil
Dash Lawrey's seasoning salt 1 teaspoon lime juice
Dash black pepper   (about ⅓ of a lime)
Dash salt

Equipment

1 very sharp carving knife 1 griddle or frying pan
1 grill

Have the butcher slice your *carne para asar* into thin sheets—about ½ inch
thick. Drape the meat onto a hot grill. (If you don't have a grill, a frying pan
should be sufficient.) Sprinkle seasoning salt, cumin, pepper, and salt onto the
meat as you barbecue it. When the meat it almost cooked, remove it from the
grill (or pan) and dice it into very small cubes. Warm the oil in a frying pan over
medium-high heat and add the diced meat and a squirt of lime juice. Stir the
meat constantly and add a bit more salt and pepper, if you like. The tiny
pieces of meat will cook very quickly, so pay attention; overcooked meat
becomes tough and chewy.

Pollo

Because chicken is the healthiest of the burrito meats, it can be enjoyed day after day without repercussion. For the burrito fanatic, this is not a minor feature. While many burrito shops prefer to grill their chicken, we have selected a recipe that calls for the chicken to be stewed, giving it a succulent tenderness. This recipe was given to us by Jose Luis "Chifora" Orosco, the head chef at Los Gallos Taqueria, who graciously spent one of his few days off in the kitchen with us. Los Gallos serves the best chicken burritos available anywhere, and Chifora gets our vote for captain of the taqueria all-star team.

Ingredients

4 boneless chicken breasts, chopped
½ onion, chopped
1 tomato
½ cup cilantro, diced
1 teaspoon granulated garlic
   (or 2 cloves garlic, diced)

1 teaspoon dried oregano
½ teaspoon ground pepper
1 teaspoon salt
4 tablespoons corn or olive oil
3–4 cups water
⅔ cup Las Palmas canned
   chile colorado

Equipment

Large pot

Frying pan

Put the chicken and water (just enough to cover) in a large pot and boil for about 20 minutes. Meanwhile, heat the oil in a frying pan and sauté the tomato, onion, garlic, oregano, cilantro, salt, and pepper over medium heat for roughly 10 minutes. Add the canned chile colorado and simmer. When the chicken is soft to the touch and can be easily pulled apart, add the sautéed tomato mixture and cook over low heat for 15 minutes, stirring occasionally. That's it! You will not be disappointed. This recipe makes enough chicken for four burritos and will keep refrigerated for about one week.

Chapter 7

Other Ingredients: Sometimes More Is Better

It would be downright un-American not to add embellishments to the great burrito waltz. While the pureness of simplicity is often comforting, it can sometimes be downright dull. Like Liberace without his jewelry, on certain days, a burrito without the extravagance of cheese, sour cream, and guacamole can seem like just another burrito.

There are several food accessories that help to round out the complete burrito experience. Chips are a necessary appetizer, and a good Mexican soft drink or fruit punch often provides just the right amount of sugar to keep you bouncing off the walls. Even if you never eat the radishes and pickled jalapeño peppers that are available only at the most authentic taquerias, they nevertheless offer visual stimulation. With a little experimentation you will have little trouble figuring out what extras make your burrito encounter just right.

The Super Burrito

Super burritos are definitely not birds or planes, but they are more powerful than a locomotive. You will never be able to leap tall buildings in a single bound after eating one. More likely, you will nap away the rest of the afternoon. And naps are a good thing. While super burritos can sometimes be excessive, more often they are the perfect tasty and caloric reminder that diets really aren't worth all the trouble.

Avocados

The avocado is one of nature's most precious gifts to mankind. The creamy flavors of this green-skinned fruit, native to Mexico and the southwestern United States, are undeniably unique and irreplaceable. As a burrito extra, raw avocados are unsurpassed. The Spanish word for the avocado, *aguacate*, was derived from the Aztec word for the pear-shaped fruit, *ahuacatl*.

Avocados grow on large broad-leafed trees. A single tree can produce ten pounds of ripe fruit a week, placing a strain on even the most committed guacamole fan's diet. Avocado trees are either male or female, with only the females producing fruit. Since it takes five years for a tree to begin to bear fruit, identifying the male trees early helps avoid future disappointment. Of the seven varieties available in the United States, the best for burrito use is the Hass avocado. The Hass was first cultivated by postman Rudolph Hass in the late 1920s, and the original tree still stands in La Habra, California. Rudy also invented junk mail, but that's another story.

Mexican and Latino markets usually sell avocados for much cheaper than the large chains, so be sure to take advantage if one is accessible to you. If you are having trouble locating an avocado vendor in your neighborhood, the California Avocado Commission, at (800) 344-4333, can assist in rectifying this most distressing deficiency.

Guacamole

One of the most prevalent burrito additives, and with good reason, is guacamole. Made from avocados and other healthy goodies, guacamole is a common complement to many Mexican dishes. In northern Mexico, a table without a bowl of the creamy green delicacy is as rare as a donkey in Manhattan. It is also a perfect chip topping, so many people prefer to serve it on the side.

There are many guacamole recipes and everyone thinks they have the best one. We can assure you confidently that they are all wrong. Our recipe will produce the best guacamole you have ever tasted. It was developed with the help of the friendly couple who run El Cacique taqueria in Los Angeles.

Ingredients

2 avocados
½ lemon
¼ cup cilantro, diced
3 cloves garlic, peeled and diced
⅛ cup white onion, diced

1 teaspoon salt
1 tablespoon juice from
   canned jalapeños
Pinch of cumin
½ medium tomato, diced

Equipment

Medium-sized bowl
Sharp knife

Fork

Cut the avocados in half, remove the pits, and scoop the soft fruit into a bowl. Squeeze the lemon juice onto the avocado. Add the garlic, onion, salt, cilantro, and jalapeño juice, and mix well with a fork. The jalapeño juice is the secret, so don't skip it. Fold in the diced tomato and a pinch of cumin. (Cumin has a very strong taste, so be careful not to add too much.) This recipe makes about 3 cups and is best served immediately after preparation.

World's Largest Burrito

The world's largest burrito was constructed in Mountain View, California, on May 3, 1997. It weighed 4,456 pounds and was 3,579 feet long. Ingredients included 123 gallons of rice, 123 gallons of beans, 84 gallons of eggs, 33 gallons of chorizo, 28 gallons of salsa, 28 gallons of sour cream, and more than 5,000 flour tortillas. It took an hour and twenty minutes to make the burrito and half an hour to weigh and measure it. Ramon Luna, who owns Burrito Real, and La Costena—both Silicon Valley burrito stalwarts—masterminded the construction. The previous record holder was built in Anaheim, California, on July 31, 1995, weighing in at a mere 4,217 pounds and measuring only 3,113 feet in length.

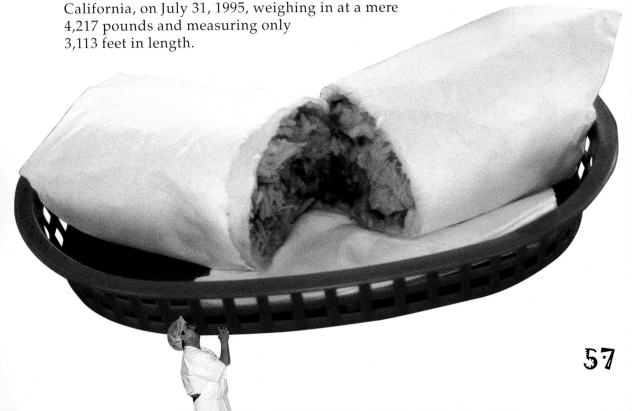

Burrito Spanish, Lesson 5
—Additional Ingredients

English	Spanish	Pronunciation
sour cream	crema	CREH-mah
cheese	queso	KEH-soh
avocado	aguacate	ah-gwah-CAH-te
orange	naranja	nah-RAHN-hah
soccer	futbol	FUHT-bohl
strawberry	fresa	FREH-sah
drink	bebida	beh-BEE-dah

Sour Cream and Cheese

Queso and *crema* are the most fattening burrito ingredients, but sometimes they add just the cool richness that a particular burrito experience needs. Many people consider them indispensable, but they're hardly exotic so further explanation is not needed. Burrito shops typically use grated Monterey Jack or Chihuahua cheese in their food.

Appetizers

Tortilla Chips

A burrito without a basket of warm tortilla chips is a moral abomination. Tortilla chips aren't exactly healthy, but as long as you use them as a tool for funneling salsa into your tummy, you'll end up eating more fruits and vegetables than chips. On the other hand, the Mexican farmers who grow the corn for these chips eat piles of them every day and live to be ninety years old. So maybe the deep-fried stuff is okay and it's office work that gives people heart attacks.

Ingredients

6 corn tortillas   1 cup vegetable or corn oil

Equipment

Frying pan   Fire extinguisher

Cut the corn tortillas into triangles, two inches per side. Get the oil good and hot but not smoking. Drop a handful of tortilla pieces into the oil. The only difficulty here is knowing when the chips are properly done. They cook fast and burn easily. When the edges start to turn light golden-brown, pull them out and lay them on a paper bag or paper towel. After they've cooled a bit, munch away.

Pickled Jalapeños

Pickled jalapeños (*jalapeños en escabeche*), often mixed with carrots and onions, are a lively and salty treat that complement many dishes. They lose some of their heat in the pickling process, and, although still hot, are surprisingly fun to eat plain. Don't be afraid; despite the long ingredients list, they are easy to make.

Ingredients

1 cup cider vinegar or
   white wine vinegar
1 tablespoon olive oil
3 teaspoons salt
1 cup water
8 jalapeños

1 carrot
⅓ white onion
3 cloves garlic, peeled
3 bay leaves
½ teaspoon whole black pepper

Equipment

Jar with screw cap (old pasta sauce jar)
Medium saucepan

Slice the peppers in half lengthwise and remove most of the seeds. Slice the carrot into thin circles, and slice the onion into quarter-inch-wide strips. Fry the garlic cloves in the olive oil for a couple of minutes in the medium saucepan and then add the carrots, onions and peppers. Continue frying for a few minutes until the onions begin to turn clear. Add the water, vinegar, bay leaves, herbs, pepper, and salt to the pot and simmer for about 10 minutes, until the carrots begin to get tender and the peppers turn brownish-green. Pour everything into the jar; cover and refrigerate at least overnight. Serve in the pickling liquid in a small bowl.

Hot Sauce

Hot sauce is salsa's younger brother. While it may at first seem difficult to distinguish between the two, it's really as easy as spotting a matador in a crowd of flight attendants. Hot sauce comes in little bottles, contains no vegetable chunks, and usually has a uniform consistency.

When religious missionaries reached the Hawaiian Islands, they found an indigenous culture so committed to enjoying the bounties of the universe they just had to put a stop to it. By demonizing beach luaus, surfing, and nakedness, they largely succeeded. Similarly, attempts were made all over the world to replace the fiery hot sauces of indigenous cuisines with the supposedly more refined European diet. Thankfully, this effort fell apart faster than the League of Nations, leaving us, today, with so many exciting, tasty, and cheap hot sauce choices, it would be impossible to list them all. The best we can do here is mention a few representative samples.

Tapatio. This easy-to-find product from Vernon, California, is very popular in the United States. With a hearty flavor and substance, it can be appreciated as much for its taste as for its heat, which is strong but not overpowering.

Tamazula. This hot sauce is definitely worth seeking out. Imported from Mexico, with a deep red color and smoky flavor, it can transform even the blandest meal into an event to remember.

Tabasco. The old standby is worth a mention as well. Ubiquitous and tasty with a strong Cajun tradition, this sauce goes with everything from apples to zebra steaks. As hot sauces go, it's fairly mild so it can be used with abandon.

Drinks

Mexico has a strong tradition of sugary and fruity drinks that often carries over into taquerias. Mexican Coke somehow tastes sweeter and less carbonated than its American counterpart, and Fanta is served everywhere in Mexico. Jarritos, a brightly colored, mildly carbonated, and delicious Mexican soft drink is widely available in the United States. Colorful roadside juice stands that serve nutritious fresh-squeezed-and-blended fruit concoctions are as common in Mexico as mini-marts are in the United States.

Carrot/Orange Juice

Aside from being good for you, this unlikely orange-colored combination tastes great. Try it and see for yourself.

Ingredients

6 fresh oranges or 2 cups orange juice   ½ cup water
2 cups diced carrots

Equipment

Blender   Strainer
Juicer (if using fresh oranges)   Pitcher

Liquefy the carrots and the water in the blender for several minutes. You may have to shake the contents at first to get it going. Strain the pulpy mass over a pitcher for about 15 minutes. Extract the juice from the oranges and mix with strained carrot juice (or just add the orange juice from concentrate). The proportion of orange to carrot juice should be about one to one, but you may wish to add slightly more orange juice. Serves two.

Strawberry Punch (Agua Fresca de Fresa)

It's authentic, frighteningly simple, sweet, delicious, and nutritious. What more could you want?

Ingredients

1 cup cold milk

1 cup water

1 cup strawberries (6 ounces)

2 tablespoons sugar

Equipment

Blender

Strainer

Combine all ingredients in blender and liquefy. Strain. Add more sugar if needed. Pour over ice and throw in a few chunks of fresh strawberry if you want. Enjoy. Walk around with a red mustache for a while just to see if anyone notices.

StraNgE Burrito Ingredients

Those of you who have been looking for a food fad to replace fondue and kiwi fruit will be pleased with the new wave of restaurants that specialize in exotic burrito ingredients, such as Thai chicken and Chinese noodles. These establishments have taken the basic burrito, added some unlikely international combinations, and renamed them wraps. A little experimentation is always a good thing, but many wraps strive so hard to be unique that they fail at just being a good burrito.

Wraps are neither an improvement nor an insult to the burrito family but rather a logical extension. They are a branch that stems from the massive trunk of the burrito's evolutionary tree. The only problem is that wraps sometimes appear to be attempting to divorce themselves from their burrito heritage. Like when an irreverent child runs away with no place to go, you know she will eventually come to her senses and return home where she belongs.

Wrap recipes are beyond the scope of this book, but if you are determined to have new flavors in your homemade burritos, get out one of your favorite Chinese/Middle-Eastern/Mediterranean/Spanish cookbooks, make one of the dishes, make or buy some flour tortillas, and follow the instructions in chapter 8.

Chapter 8
How to Build and Eat the Perfect Burrito: Instructions for People Who Never Read Instructions

Why does Radio Shack even bother to print its twenty-three-page digital clock/radio manual? The pictures of little skulls, bold-faced exclamation marks, and lightning bolts can be mildly amusing, but it would be more realistic if the directions said simply: 1. Throw away instructions; 2. Unwrap clock; 3. Plug in clock; 4. Randomly press all of the buttons until you decide you can't figure out how to set the clock; 5. Dig instructions out of garbage and start over. Spare yourself the agony of droopy, lopsided burritos with leaky tortillas, and admit to yourself that, while you are intelligent, graceful, and clever, certain tasks are simply easier to accomplish with some guidance.

Many great burritos teeter between gastronomic nirvana and a gooey pile of mishmash. Making a bit of a mess is part of the burrito-eating experience, but silverware should never be a necessity. Keep in mind that cooperation is the reigning philosophy among a great burrito's ingredients. Like people, when burrito ingredients learn to accept and get along with one another, a festive harmony ensues. The beans mingle effortlessly with the rice and meat while the salsa spreads itself around like spiked punch at a high school dance.

This chapter is devoted to the creation of the ultimate homemade burrito. The knowledge you have gained from previous chapters, coupled with a little common sense and these simple instructions (plus a few ingredients and a kitchen), is all you should need.

Step 1—Burrito beginnings

Have a sense of humor. Open a bottle of wine. Relax.

Step 2—Preliminaries

Make some salsa fresca and buy (or make) some tortilla chips. This is the perfect appetizer and will keep you going throughout the burrito construction process. Try not to eat all the salsa because you will need some for your burrito.

Step 3—What do I want in my burrito?

Look over the following ingredient list and decide which to include in your home-cooked bundle of love. We recommend starting with the salsa fresca, beans, rice, and carne asada or chicken, but by all means experiment with different combinations and discover your favorites. You may want to buy the tortillas on your first attempt; Sonoran-style 12-inch are best.

Tortillas	Whole avocado
Salsa	Cheese
Meat	Sour cream
Beans	Diced lettuce,
Rice	cilantro, or onions
Guacamole	Other?

Step 4—The Assessment

Critically assess both your cooking skills and your kitchen equipment. Having access to all of the hardware available at Le Cordon Bleu might allow an average cook to prepare an exceptional meal, but if you consider any of the Chef Boyardee products to be home cooking, a rack of assorted whisks probably won't have much impact on your final product. Learn to accept your equipment and aptitude limitations and decide which burrito components to buy and which to cook.

Step 5—Hunt, gather, cook

Assemble the burrito components of your choice and lay them out on the counter. Marvel at their beauty.

Step 6—Siesta

Your first full burrito creation is about to take form. Take a break. Put some Mariachi Vargas in the CD player, dig that sombrero out of your closet, and do a little dance. Open the window shades and turn up the volume on your stereo. Entertain your neighbors.

Step 7—Screwing your head on straight

Remember not to expect perfection on your first try. Keep your expectations low and you won't be so disappointed if your burrito explodes all over the carpet.

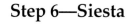

Step 8—The basic assembly

Take one of your flour tortillas and give it a light grilling—about 20 seconds per side. If you are adding cheese to your burrito, this is the time to do it. Grated Monterey Jack is best. Don't worry if it doesn't all melt; the other ingredients will take care of that. While the tortilla is grilling, try to recall your happiest childhood memory. Place the warm tortilla on a flat surface on top of a square sheet of tinfoil that is slightly larger than the tortilla. Scoop a large spoonful of rice into an eye-shaped pile across the middle of the tortilla. Lay an equal amount of beans over the top of the rice; a little bean liquid adds flavor, but too much can cause trouble. Dump a couple of spoonfuls of meat onto the side of the pile that is closest to you.

Step 9—Spice it up

Spread some salsa over the top of the pile. How much you use is up to you, but we recommend at least equal parts with the meat. Salsa is as integral to a burrito as frosting is to a birthday cake, so lay on a healthy dose of fiery goodness. If you're not adding extras, skip ahead to step 11.

Step 10—These extras all have speaking parts

Avocado slices are almost a secret ingredient because so many people who should know better neglect to include them. Place three or four lengthwise slices of avocado on top of your growing pile. If desired, scoop some sour cream and guacamole into the mix. Skip the guacamole if you have added raw avocado or vice versa. If the diet police show up at this stage, be strong. Believe in yourself and affirm that you can have your burrito exactly how you want it regardless of calories.

Step 11—You're ready to roll

Here comes the big event—the roll-up. Even if you've done well so far, it is still possible to blow the whole thing with improper rolling technique. Remember step 1. Shrug your shoulders a few times, wiggle your head around, and push up your sleeves. Pick up the far edge of the tortilla and lift it so all the ingredients shift towards you. Drop the far edge and fold the sides in about 2 inches so that the ingredients will not fall out of the ends of the burrito. Simultaneously, with your thumbs, fold the front edge of the tortilla away from you, tucking it underneath the ingredients. Concentrate on keeping the tortilla tight as you roll, and continue to push in the sides. When fully rolled, slide the bulging mass toward the front third of the sheet of tin foil. Very quickly, roll the burrito up in the foil, as tightly as possible, like a carpet. Crinkle the foil around the ends of the burrito.

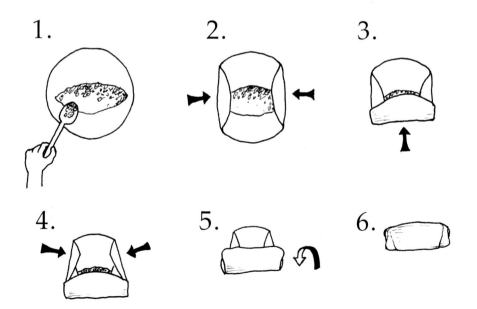

12 Step 12— Congratulations!

Pat yourself on the back. Your creation is now ready to meet its maker.

13 Step 13—Eating the burrito (almost)

Wait! Before you dive in, it is important to make sure that you have the table set correctly. Always have a bowl of salsa and a basket of chips with your burrito. To drink, try some Mexican beer (Dos Equis or Pacifico are good), a Jarritos, or one of the fruit drinks in chapter 7. Pickled jalapeños are always a welcome complement.

14 Step 14—Eating the burrito (we mean it this time)

Okay, if you've made it this far, either you have amazing self-control or you ate the whole bag of chips while you were cooking. Dig in, but don't be a rookie and peel off all the foil you just rolled on. Strip it away in sections, taking off only enough to allow for big healthy bites. This will help the burrito maintain its form for as long as possible. You'll probably still make a mess, but at least it will be a controlled mess.

15 Step 15—A time to reflect

People who have never experienced a spiritual sentiment in their entire lives have been known to sit and reflect for a moment after finishing a warm, freshly wrapped burrito. Try it. Briefly consider making another burrito, but then realize that eating anything more is really a physical impossibility.

Step 16—Siesta number two (why not?)

Take a nap and leave the cleanup for another day.

Burrito break in downtown Manhattan.

Chapter 9
Burrito P.I.:
How to Detect a Quality Taqueria

Like burritos, taquerias come in all shapes and sizes. There are roadside taquerias in Mexico that would have a hard time passing for a fourth-grade clubhouse, and there are grandiose, sterile corporate monsters created by slick marketing guys and a squadron of interior decorators. While each may have its own unique character and may even dish out memorable burrito flavors, the profile of the ideal taqueria—with promise for exquisite burritos— rests somewhere in between.

Spotting a good place requires a delicate combination of skill and luck, strength and control, intelligence and instinct. By reducing your dependence on luck and sharpening your investigative instincts, this chapter will insure that you are buying your burritos at the best possible establishment. If you run into any trouble along the way, put on your best Hawaiian print shirt and ask yourself, What would Tom Selleck do in this situation?

Theoretical Framework Developed by Really Smart Science Guys

Burrito restaurants can be classified into four simple categories and plotted on a handy graph as detailed below. To avoid confusion in the future, a copy of this graph should be kept in a highly visible place—perhaps taped to your bicycle handlebars or bathroom mirror.

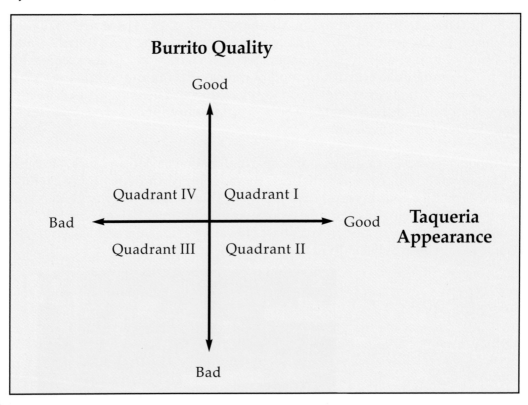

Do not be alarmed by the apparent complexity of this diagram. Keep in mind that, with perseverance and determination, even the authors were able to figure out what it means. It was developed for your benefit by really smart science guys, the same science guys who developed the Flo-Bee, the Nordic-Track, and Ginsu knives.

Restaurants that fall in quadrant I serve up quality burritos in exquisite surroundings. Being as rare as the sun in Chicago, quadrant I taquerias are always a welcome find (see chapter 10 for examples). Because they are suitable for parents, casual dates, and out-of-town guests, the discovery of a quadrant I taqueria will insure that you never have to skip your daily burrito due to nagging social engagements.

Quadrant II taquerias look promising, have an interesting menu, a friendly atmosphere, and food that makes you wish you had grabbed the leftover casserole out of the fridge instead. Short of a run-in with a swarm of angry bees, there is no greater disappointment for the burrito connoisseur than an encounter with a quadrant II taqueria. Establishments with big reputations and strong name recognition occasionally slip into this category, getting so accustomed to being a big player in the global burrito trade that they forget what got them there in the first place. (For more on this topic, see Marlon Brando, page 86.)

Taquerias that fall into quadrant III often resemble fast-food joints and produce burritos akin to those available beneath the heat lamps at 7-11. It is unclear why ugly restaurants that dish out disastrous food are not swiftly eliminated from the food chain. Proliferation of these terrible wastes of space in our cities proves that Darwin's principles of evolution are not applicable to the restaurant business. Quadrant III taquerias are often open at odd hours, making them seem like the perfect solution for late-night munchies after a few too many beers with your pals . . . until you wake up the next morning thinking there is a small logging operation going on inside your body.

Quadrant IV establishments, which are the most elusive for the novice burrito hunter, look like communist-era border checkpoints but still manage to produce delicious burritos. They should be cherished like that last Valium at a family reunion. A wobbly chair crammed into the corner of a windowless concrete room can become quite charming when the burritos taste great. Engineers, economists, and other style-impaired types are particularly appreciative of the no-nonsense efficiency of quadrant IV taquerias.

When in doubt about a taqueria, remember the graph. Then kick yourself for all those times in high school geometry when you said, I'll never use this in the real world.

A thorough taqueria investigation, however, requires much more than broad general feelings or seemingly arbitrary graphs. The distinct characteristics of a taqueria should be broken into definitive categories and inspected and interpreted individually.

Neighborhood—Mr. Rogers Doesn't Live Here

While acceptable burritos can be found everywhere from country clubs to office complexes, more promising burritos tend to congregate, quite naturally, in neighborhoods with a heavy Latino influence. Indications of fertile burrito territory include Spanish signs, grocery stores that sell piñatas, murals painted on buildings, and outdoor fruit stands. Even if Latinos had not developed a particular propensity for burrito cooking, these vibrant and bustling neighborhoods would still be ideal spots for burrito consumption.

The following table gives some helpful examples of good and bad burrito territories:

Good Burrito Territory	Bad Burrito Territory
Mission District, San Francisco	Sun City, Arizona
Adams-Morgan District, Washington, DC	Skowheegan, Maine
South Tucson, Arizona	New Brunswick, Canada
East Los Angeles	Singapore
Albuquerque, New Mexico	Bloomfield Hills, Michigan
Rogers Park, Chicago	Bismarck, North Dakota
Imuris, Mexico	Linden, Kansas

Burrito Spanish, Lesson 6—At the Taqueria

English	Spanish	Pronunciation
This burrito is delicious	Esto burrito es delicioso	ES-toh boo-RREE-toh es del-ee-see-OH-soh
to go / for here	para llevar / para aqui	PAHR-ah yeh-VAR / PAHR-ah ah-KEE
please / thank you	por favor / gracias	pohr fah-VOHR / GRAH-see-ahs
see you later	hasta luego	AHS-tah LWEH-goh
Selena	Selena	Seh-LEH-nah

A Burrito Patent?

Eddie Bernal, of Taco Operations, Inc., actually holds patents on a Method of Making a Readily Portable Burrito, (US 4491601) and a more elusive Readily Portable Food Item. A patent has also been issued to Mr. Bernal on the Readily Portable Burrito (US 4399156). It precisely describes the method for rolling and folding (in a counterclockwise fashion) the tortilla around a stick—sort of a burrito popsicle.

Architecture—From Handmade Adobe to Cheap Stucco Hell

Taqueria architecture falls somewhere between the spacious functionality of Protestant reformation structures and Las Vegas hotel design. Some taquerias are exquisitely manicured, while others have a striking resemblance to the tool-shed you and your dad built in the backyard when you were eight years old. Some occupy windowed storefronts, and some are nothing more than a wooden cart full of ingredients.

Taquerias have an amazing ability to adapt to their physical environment. Like hermit crabs taking over abandoned shells, they have the capacity to take root in any type of building without much modification. They are able to make a seamless transformation from burger-flipping Foster's Freeze to burrito-rolling taqueria with the same nimble elegance of a caterpillar turning into a butterfly.

The most important (and sometimes the only notable) aspect of a taqueria's outward appearance is its sign, which gives valuable insight into the character of the restaurant inside. Hand-painted red-and-green letters on the front window or facade of a taqueria are particularly promising, and the use of the festive taqueria font, which uses all capital letters with colored shadowing and rounded characters, is almost a sure indication of quality burritos. Handwritten specials, posted in the window among neon Budweiser signs, usually precede tasty burritos. Their faded green paper, however, is a dead giveaway—these specials have always been and will always be the daily specials.

Interior Decor—More Fun Than a Live Eel in Your Shorts

The interiors of great taquerias are usually the result of piecemeal efforts by the family who owns and runs the business, taking the rejected objects from their friends' homes and arranging them as randomly as possible inside. The amalgamation of strangeness that is formed by the seemingly misplaced decorations somehow manages to create the perfect burrito-eating environment. Trying too hard to make the interior look Mexican or authentic has an effect exactly opposite to that which was intended; it ends up feeling contrived.

Interior Item	What it Means
Posters of Mexico	You need a vacation
Cheap-looking or tacky, random artwork	Owners have been to Tijuana
Strange lighting fixtures	Taqueria was once home to a German restaurant
Religious symbols	Burrito is blessed by God
Soccer on TV	You will be entertained by screaming announcers
Calendars	Can record the number of consecutive days you have eaten a burrito
Mismatched chairs	You could be back in a dorm lounge
	Original set broken during drunken soccer argument
Dried peppers on the wall	They looked good when they were new—15 years ago
Any type of mural or painting directly on the wall	Michelangelo was here
Random paper signs explaining funky dishes taped to any flat surface	You will read them all and then order something plain
Strange-looking plastic clocks that never tell the right time	Who cares what time it is back at the office?
Picture of Pancho Villa	We all need more danger and romance in our lives
Taqueria has less than four walls	You're probably in Mexico
Gumball machine	We have no idea
Beer poster with bikini babes	Beer makes you a man

Aside from the list above, there are several distinct items that are almost always accounted for in taquerias that serve delicious burritos. They include a carrot juicer, a jukebox, hanging garlic, references to soccer, and beer paraphernalia. Also watch for candy dispensers and a well-stocked upright soda cooler.

83

Clientele—Shepherds in a World of Sheep

The best burrito spots are frequented by a clientele as diverse as the crowd at a United Nations ice cream social. Students, professionals, locals, gen-x bike messenger types, construction workers, Mexican families, and retirees eat together, sharing the healthy glow of a little tortilla spirituality, and proving by the smiles on their faces that quality burritos do not discriminate.

Sometimes, very specific clues about the burritos can be gathered from the clientele. For example, a taqueria that caters almost exclusively to college students is likely to have food that is good compared to the college cafeteria but seems a bit lackluster to anyone whose tastebuds haven't been hammered into submission by the food service gestapo. At least the place will have cheap prices, late hours, and a tolerance for boisterous drunks.

Taquerias that are full of dressy business people will probably be churning out a General Motors assembly line of burritos using healthy, fresh ingredients and incorporating trendy flavors. Positive aspects include speed, convenience, and cleanliness. The drawback is that the burrito will be as exciting as a two-week tax-law seminar.

As a burrito joint falls closer to the realm of a formal restaurant and further from the informal world of taquerias, the diversity of the clientele, along with the quality of the burrito, tends to decline. In fact, you probably only have two salsa options at restaurants like this: mild or extra-mild. A couple of fresh jalapeños slipped into an unknowing customer's burrito would be disastrous. Of course, everyone is free to choose how much excitement they want from their food, but excitement is kind of like clean air, and why anyone would want less than the maximum is beyond understanding.

Employees—No Gringos Allowed

Clad in matching blue, red, or green T-shirts, the employees at the best burrito restaurants in the world can be either men or women, but they are almost always Latino. It is unclear why humans with roots south of the border possess such a heightened sense of burrito perfection, but it is also unclear why full-grown adults would go to blows over a Tickle-Me Elmo doll. Anybody with sufficient knowledge and ambition should be capable of making a truly great burrito, but we've rarely seen anybody without Latino ancestry and a good attitude do it professionally. Those of us with a serious burrito dependency can only thank a benevolent universe for making good attitudes and Latino ancestry a common combination.

More important than where they're from, however, is how great burrito builders approach their work. Burritos respond to *activity*. They're the Frankenstein Monster of food—you can't just patch one together; you have to bring it to life. When employees stand behind the counter like a bunch of contented farm animals, the resulting burrito will sit there with all the zest and life of a steamed eggplant. But when there's some vitality behind the counter, when the pitter-patter of Spanish, sizzling meat, mariachi music, and laughter combine in an energizing rumble, the burritos will come alive.

Menu—The Mealtime Rosetta Stone

The presentation of a menu is almost as important as the content. Aside from a coherent basic menu board, quality taquerias like to post makeshift signs that announce specials and super items. Establishments that exhibit this type of spontaneity are undoubtedly operated by creative improvisers. Their approach to burritos cannot be restrained by a static menu board.

Hoping you know what you want before you walk through the door, a few taquerias don't even bother to post a menu board. Chances are, the workers do not speak a word of English, so unless you are prepared to eat a tripe burrito, you'd better come equipped with your best improvisational sign-language skills (or study up on your burrito Spanish lessons).

Marlon Brando Burrito Syndrome

One must be careful when judging a taqueria by the size of its crowd. It's possible that the place no longer has anything to offer, but it hangs around through the strength of its reputation. By all objective measures, the product has abandoned its former glory and sunk into shameful decline. People should have stopped paying attention years ago but somehow the place continues to get press coverage and crowds. As painful as it may be to see this, we must have the courage to recognize the truth.

The following table will help aspiring Burrito P.I.s interpret important menu items.

Item that should be present in a good taqueria	What it means
Jarritos (Mexican soda)	Sugar from Mexico is just as sweet, but the food coloring is five times stronger
Negro Modelo, Dos Equis, Corona (Mexican beer)	Even if the burritos are bad, you can at least get drunk
Chorizo (sausage)	Meat can be served in more ways than you ever dreamed
Fresh carrot juice	Great burritos You can improve your eyesight while enjoying a burrito
Fresh avocado	Almost as good as winning the lottery
Choice of different kinds of rice	Doesn't matter. They're either all good or all bad
Free chips	Owners adhere to the Taqueria Bill of Rights
Salsa bar	You won't have to beg for extra salsa Owners understand that chips are just an excuse to eat salsa
Pickled carrots, pickled peppers, and radishes	Great burritos You will eat one out of curiosity

Strong taquerias also have a fairly standard list of non-burrito food items on their menus:

1. Quesadillas—more authentic than you think
2. Tacos—burritos' smaller, and therefore cheaper, cousins
3. Carne asada plate—the meat-lover's dream
4. Enchiladas—dripping heart attacks waiting to happen
5. Tortas—almost a burrito but with grilled bread instead of a tortilla

Suspect menu items include the following:

1. Cheeseburgers
2. Ballpark-style Nachos
3. Hot Dogs
4. Pizza
5. Mashed potatoes

Music—Burrito Beats with Your Burrito Treats

A solid jukebox filled with excellent Mexican music is vital to a successful taqueria. Jukeboxes at the best taquerias always have three compact discs magically rotating above the selection buttons. Their purpose is uncertain, but they are rumored to be part of a complex alien communication ring.

The following list should be considered essential to any great taqueria's jukebox:

1. Mariachi Vargas—been around (with a rotating line-up) since the early 1900s.
2. Vicente Fernandez—Mexican crooner a la Frank Sinatra.
3. Pepe Aguilar—son of equally famous mariachi singer Antonio Aguilar.
4. Pedro Infante—prolific songster whose compositions are often performed by others.
5. Pedro Vargas—romantic boleros from the '40s and '50s with orchestras.
6. Jose Jimenez—wrote and performed many popular songs.
7. Los Tigres Del Norte—widely known Norteño group with some success in the U.S.
8. Javier Solis—passionate ranchera and mariachi singer.
9. Juan Gabriel—pop ballads, Mexican style.

How to Tell if a Taqueria is Right for You

The Cross-Town Test

Ask yourself the question, Given all of the food options available to me, am I eager to *cross town* to retrieve a burrito from _____? Any tortilla-wrapped bundle that passes this test is surely a fine product.

The Daydream Test

The daydream test digs deeper into the spiritual side of the burrito-lover's consciousness. While you are sitting at your desk, waiting for lunchtime to arrive, do you struggle to keep fantasies about a certain taqueria out of your head? Do you find yourself thinking that an hour and forty-five minutes hasn't seemed so impossibly long since your mother dragged you to see *Yentl?* That's the daydream test, and the burrito is undoubtedly worth the wait.

Instructions are for Losers

After taking the neighborhood, building exterior, decor, clientele, employees, and menu into account, the burrito connoisseur must turn inward and ask his/her conscience, How does it *feel?* There is an intangible element that cannot be captured through analysis, and the power of one's intuition should never be underestimated. Don't listen to your head; let your stomach and your sense of adventure lead you to a great spot. And if it's a disaster, well, that's a good story too.

Chapter 10
The World's Best Burritos: The Joy of Not Cooking

After eating nothing but burritos for months, many of our friends expected us to be quite sick of them. Not so! Had we the time and sufficient funds, we would happily head out on the trail for another lap around the country. But we have already found many more great taquerias than we can include in this book. This chapter pays tribute to the supreme examples of taqueria artistry and explores what makes them such significant landmarks along the trail of the little burro.

This chapter will certainly result in some bruised feelings and ugly thoughts on the part of burrito connoisseurs who feel we have neglected their favorite spot. As a worst-case scenario, we may find ourselves trying to rent a room from Salmon Rushdie. We came by our decisions honestly and will let the burritos speak for themselves.

El Farolito Taqueria
2779 Mission St., San Francisco, California, (415) 824-7877

It is no longer a secret that El Farolito consistently builds some of the best (and cheapest—$2.45) burritos on the planet; the line of well-pierced hipsters, families, and suited businessmen stretches out the door until 3:00 A.M. almost every night. In fact, everything on their menu is superb, and, despite the hectic pace, the service is always efficient. Of curious interest is El Farolito's total disdain for basic economic theory. Despite a continuous capacity crowd and premium product, the prices are on the low end of the local scale. For fear of ruining a good thing, it is probably best to not explore the reasons behind this phenomenon.

The *al pastor* burrito at Farolito is heavenly, the *carne asada* is tender, and the *pollo* good, although it can sometimes be a bit dry. The super burritos are heavy on the sour cream but have, nevertheless, inspired grown men to weep tears of joy. For a clinic in burrito building, pay attention as the maroon-shirted gentlemen behind the counter roll out perfectly formed specimens in under ten seconds. Despite their sometimes overwhelming hotness, the salsas at El Farolito are exceptional and are a featured recipe in chapter 4. Fantasize that you are a taqueria worker as you ladle out your own cupful from behind the counter.

The occasional wandering crazy guy and walk-in-closet size combine to make El Farolito a hard-core burrito fan's delight. There is virtually no separation between the dining room and the kitchen, and the don't-even-try style of interior decoration feels appropriate alongside one of the busiest intersections in San Francisco. The jukebox often blares cheesy Mexican love songs loud enough to make conversation impossible.

Mr. Salvador Lopez, the well-dressed founder of El Farolito, moved to San Francisco from Mexico City, where he had worked in a popular restaurant of the same name. He spent seven years mastering the art of burrito cookery behind the counter at El Castillito Taqueria in San Francisco before opening the doors to his own taqueria in 1982. Having achieved the status of burrito powerbroker, Mr. Lopez now oversees his three-restaurant empire from the plush comfort of the El Farolito Bar next door. After some initial reluctance, he revealed to us that the secret behind El Farolito's astounding success is a magic grill, rumored to have been found at the foot of a rainbow amid the treacherous peaks of the Sierra Madre. When asked what makes a good burrito, Mr. Lopez responded, grinning in typically calm, smooth, modest, and elusive fashion, "I don't know—everything."

El Tepeyac Cafe

812 N. Evergreen Ave., Los Angeles, California, (213) 268-1960

With a reputation that extends throughout Southern California, El Tepeyac is truly an institution. The customers that line up daily to quench their burrito thirst are so loyal that owner Manuel Rojas could probably start his own church. The legacy of El Tepeyac will not be fading anytime soon; Manuel's son Pancho, who grew up in the restaurant, opened a second eatery in 1992 in Monterey Park, California.

Manuel's Special, with over five pounds' worth of ingredients that fill two tortillas to near bursting, is the Mount Everest of burritos. It was created when Manny bet someone that they could not finish one of his burritos. He won. Many of the burritos at El Tepeyac are named after Manny's favorite customers. The Okie, for example, was named after a country-boy regular from Idaho who liked his burritos a certain way. The machaca burrito at El Tepeyac might be the single-best reason for visiting Southern California. It shows an unusual degree of character and depth for a burrito composed of only meat, eggs, cheese, and a tortilla.

While Manny's relentless chatter and undeniable character help to keep the atmosphere inside his restaurant festive, El Tepeyac's suburban location in the heart of heavily Latino East Los Angeles gives the burrito experience an undeniable aura of authenticity. The kitchen is frantic and noisy, and the sizzling excitement usually manages to spill over into the smiles on the customers' faces.

Customer waiting in line to eat: We've been eating here for twenty-five years.
Us: Has it changed?
Customer: One thing hasn't changed and that's the line out front.

When we asked how long the restaurant had been around, Manuel replied without blinking, "Since yesterday morning." In reality, the Rojas family has been running various restaurants in the Los Angeles area since 1931. El Tepeyac began as an ice-cream shop in the garage of the Rojas home where local kids used to sip milkshakes and listen to the jukebox. Food was introduced, Manuel's father did some remodeling on the garage, and the establishment began its transformation into a full-scale restaurant. The business has remained a family affair ever since. In typical sarcastic fashion, Manny recounted his restaurant's history for us: "My mom was the boss for forty-three years, but she died and now my daughter is boss. I'm a slave."

Los Gallos Taqueria

3726 Florence St. (in the Marsh Manor Shopping Center),
Redwood City, California, (650) 369-1864

Los Gallos, where we've eaten over 150 times, is without a doubt our favorite taqueria. As the birthplace of this book, it also holds a special place in our hearts. Viviana, who runs the register with alarming efficiency, is probably the real boss of the operation (you're a real charmer if you can get her to smile—go ahead, try it). On the other hand, if you can get manager Juan, the world's most cheerful man, to stop smiling, we'll buy you a burrito. Interestingly, all of the workers at Los Gallos are originally from the Mexican town of San Jose de Gracia. Though we've never visited that city, we can only imagine how amazing the food is.

97

A Los Gallos burrito is about as close to perfect as food gets. The tortillas are always supple, the meats are juicy and tender, the beans and rice play their parts perfectly, and the salsas taste downright otherworldly. Even the chips are unbeatable. The burritos are laced with a flavorful richness that is unequaled in the taqueria world. Jose Luis "Chifora" Orosco, the main chef, has been working in taquerias for over eleven years, and it shows. He started off in San Francisco's Mission District, before making Los Gallos his home. Don't miss his astoundingly delicious regular chicken burrito.

In a ubiquitous strip-mall setting, Los Gallos is flanked by a charming hardware store/laundromat combo. It's located in Silicon Valley, an area famous for nerdy young millionaires and jobs where the average corporate drone commands more technology than James Bond. Surprisingly, these hungry computer jockeys have combined with a large Latino community to produce a thriving burrito culture.

Its name a tribute to owner Miguel Jimenez's affinity for cock fighting, Los Gallos opened its doors seven years ago in San Mateo, California. When the neighboring shopping mall went the way of the dodo bird in 1995, Mr. Jimenez moved his operation to its present site. One year later, with business thriving, they annexed the adjacent store and transformed it into a cavernous dining room. Happily, this also made room for a jukebox and gumball machine. So the next time you're power-lunching with the world's high-tech mavericks, prove yourself a savvy insider and suggest a meeting at Los Gallos.

Taqueria Cancun
2288 Mission St., San Francisco, California, (415) 252-9560

Taqueria Cancun is in many ways what the burrito experience was meant to be—cheap enough to be paid for in change, colorful enough to put a smile on your face, and delicious enough to keep you coming back time after time. The neighborhood is grungy but full of character and culture, and you'll likely dine among purple-haired punkers, middle-aged plumbers, drunk twenty-something scenesters, and middle-class suburbanites.

Tight construction and perfect ingredient integration make the burritos at Cancun an engineering marvel. They are some of the biggest we've seen, but because they're so tasty, it's difficult *not* to finish one. The super burrito at Cancun is the best we've had, with enough extras to add flavor but not so many as to overwhelm the main ingredients. There isn't a weak spot on the menu, so any ingredient combination will be satisfying; but don't forget to ask for fresh avocado slices in your burrito.

According to co-owners Gerardo Rico and Pedro Grande, Taqueria Cancun wasn't exactly a success right away—on their first day in business they served only one lunch. It didn't take an MBA to diagnose the problem—the street gangs that loitered in the doorway and grafitied the tables kept even the most rabid burrito fanatics away. With an integrated program of diplomacy, aesthetic improvements, and a no-nonsense and persistent attitude, the new taqueria moguls convinced the gang members to move on. Cancun is now one of the most charming taquerias in San Francisco with a relaxed, satisfied clientele and cheerful employees.

TAQUERIA CAN-CU

2288 Mission Street at 19th Street
San Francisco, CA • (415) 252-9560
WELCOME • (TAX NOT INCLUDED) • BIENVENIDOS

BURRITO 2.75
Any meat, rice, beans, onions, cilantro, salsa.

VEGETARIAN BURRITO 2.75
Rice, beans, cheese, onions, cilantro, salsa, sour cream, avocado

SUPER BURRITO 3.88
Your choice of meat, rice, beans, onions, cilantro, salsa, cheese, avocado & sour cream.

BURRITO MOJADO (A BIG ONE) ONLY 3.88
Your choice of meat, rice, beans, onions, cilantro, salsa, topped with ehchilada sauce, guacamole, melted cheese, sour cream, tomato & salsa.

BURRITAS 2.75
Two flour tortillas, ham & cheese.

TACO 1.65
Two soft tortillas, your choice of meat, onions, onions, cilantro, & Salsa.

TORTAS 2.75
A french roll bone with your choice of meat, refried beans, onions, tomato, cheese, sour cream & avocado.

CHOICE OF MEATS

CARNE ASADA / GRILLED STEAK
AL PASTOR / MARINATED PORK
POLLO / CHICKEN
CHORIZO / MEXICAN SAUSAGE
LENGUA / BEEF TONGUE
CABEZA / BEEF HEAD
SESOS / BEEF BRAINS

SPECIALTIES

CARNE ASADA 4.80
Grilled beef steak, rice, beans, salsa & tortillas.

ENCHILADAS (2) ...3.95
Rice, beans, sour cream & tortillas.

ALAMBRES 4.80
Chunks of beef steak, onions, mild peppers, bacon, rice, beans & tortillas.

EXTRA CHIPS 0.75
CEBOLLITAS (grilled onions) .1.25
EXTRA MEAT 1.00

DRINKS

AGUAS FRESCAS 0.85
(natural fruit drinks)
SODAS 0.85
MEXICAN SODAS 1.35
JUICE 2.00
(Fresh squeezed, orange or carrot)
COFFEE 0.55
MEXICAN BEER 1.85
AMERICAN BEER 1.35

QUESA

SUIZA
Flour tortilla
& carne asad

PECHU

SUIZA
Flour tortilla
& grilled chic

QUESA
Corn tortilla

QUESA
Flour tortilla

SUPER
Corn chips, m
cream, avoca
(With choice

NACHO
Corn chips, m
refried beans

EGGS
Scrambled wi

SHRIM
(Coctel de Ca

LA

. . . . .2.75

d cheese

d beef).

. . . . .2.75

d cheese

LA (CORN) . .1.15

ed cheese.

LA (FLOUR) . .1.65

ed cheese.

CHOS 3.75

heese, refried beans, sour

camole, salsa & jalapeños .

t, add $1.)

REGULAR) 2.75

cheese,

peños.

STYLE . .3.75

rizo or ham or hot salsa.

OCKTAIL .4.95

es) ¡RIQUISIMO!

After purchasing their first restaurant from a former employer, Gerardo and Pedro, with only two other employees, put in fourteen-hour days as they built their business. Today, the pair cultivates employees that share their passion, instructing chefs to cook as if they were cooking for themselves. Food processors are not used at Cancun because, according to Gerardo, "cooking is in the hands." Summing up our burrito philosophy quite nicely, he added, "Love is a very important burrito ingredient. Love for the food. Love for people. If you make it without love, it's no good." Senor Rico claims no ill will towards any burrito, no matter how pedestrian, although he is quick to add that frozen burritos are for emergencies only. One of the secrets behind the delicious food at Cancun is Gerardo's self-proclaimed ability to detect poor-quality ingredients with his hypersensitive stomach. Aside from that, Gerardo made it clear that in the taqueria world, good people do finish first, saying, "We do things right around here—honestly. Because that way I can sleep well at night."

Taco Loco

44 Broadway, Somerville, Massachusetts, (617) 625-3830

Somewhere in New England we lost the trail of the little burro. After some disastrous burritos in Providence, Rhode Island, we checked our compass and headed toward the studenty environs of Boston. And there we found Taco Loco, a lonely outpost of burrito culture in the cold of New England. Taco Loco serves the best burritos in Boston. The robust ingredients and

voluptuous salsa mark this operation as a citadel of burrito authenticity, with a product that exudes a fresh and flavorful wholeness that is the result of thoughtful preparation and kitchen expertise.

In fact, husband-and-wife owners Tony and Blanca (Blanci) Morales honed their cooking skills in Mexican restaurants for fifteen years before opening their own business in 1996. They based their burrito philosophy around customization, saying that their customers should have whatever they want, not what some chef wants to cook. Because they prefer to let the fundamental ingredients shine through, Tony and Blanca keep their recipes simple, without too many over-powering spices. It comes as no surprise to learn that Tony holds a master's degree in theology—he undoubtedly injects a portion of spiritual wholeness into every burrito sold at Taco Loco.

Taco Loco's Somerville location is perfectly suited to burritos. The urban blue-collar neighborhood is not particularly safe at night, and the potholed streets are covered with rusty old Chevy pickups. The restaurant's petite interior is ringed by a small counter and colorful murals, and the tiny kitchen upstairs behind the counter gives the place a homey personal feel. The Moraleses gave Taco Loco its name because they felt the word *loco*, meaning crazy or out of the ordinary, would describe their lively food well. We think they have chosen wisely—their burritos are anything but run-of-the-mill.

El Cuervo

110 West Washington St., San Diego, California (619) 295-9713

The long red carpet that leads to the register in the back of the restaurant is a fitting preamble to a burrito experience at El Cuervo. The burritos are elegant, the service friendly, the atmosphere authentic, and the clientele excited and boisterous.

The burritos at El Cuervo, as is the case with many Southern Californian burritos, are made with beans and meat, or just meat. El Cuervo manages to turn this simplicity into a positive by using the best possible ingredients. The tortillas are fresh and the colorful salsa is a particularly inspired blend of carrots, tomatoes, peppers, and spices. Though the burritos are not particularly large, the prices on the extensive menu are unbelievably low.

The massive murals that consume a large portion of the walls at El Cuervo are, aside from the tasty food, its most distinguishing feature. Plastic plants dangle above wooden octagonal tables with high-backed chairs, and a huge rack of gumball machines beckon for your spare change as you depart through the wrought-iron screen door.

Sergio, son of founder Jose Barajas, has brightened the kitchen at El Cuervo with his managerial smile for over fifteen years. Mr. Barajas and his other son, Ricardo, are co-owners. While Jose quietly insures that the kitchen staff is dishing out awe-inspiring heaps of *carne asada*, Ricardo takes care of the books and keeps the crowd of lunch-hour desperados from running amok.

El Cuervo
TACO SHOP
110 West Washington St.
San Diego, CA
295-9713
★

Chips & Guacamole

Sm. $1.35   Lg. $1.80

OPEN 7 DAYS A WEEK
Delicious Mexican Food To Go

} MENUDO
Saturday
and
Sunday }

5 Rolled Taquitos w/Guacamole, Lettuce, Tomatoes & Cheese $2.25

COMBINATIONS

#1 Cheese Enchilada, Beef Taco,
Rice & Beans 4.59
#2 Chile Relleno, Cheese Enchilada,
Rice or Beans & Salad 4.39
#3 2 Cheese Enchiladas, Rice & Beans
Guacamole Salad 4.69
#4 Beef Taco, Cheese Enchilada,
Rice or Beans, Bean Tostada 4.79
#5 2 Chicken Enchiladas w/Sour Cream,
Rice & Beans 4.89
#6 Mixed Burrito, Guacamole, Salad
plus Rice & Beans 4.39
#7 Order of Machaca, plus
Rice & Beans 4.95
#8 Chorizo with Egg,
Rice & Beans 4.95
#9 Order of Carne Asada with
Rice & Beans 4.95
#10 Chimichanga, Rice & Beans 4.95
#11 Shredded Beef Tacos,
side of Rice & Beans 4.59
#12 Chile Relleno, Tamale,
Rice & Beans 4.69
#13 Carnitas,
Rice & Beans 4.95

TACOS

Carne Asada Taco 1.75
Bean Taco 1.00
Beef 1.50
Hamburger 1.30
Chicken 1.50
Guacamole 1.00
Rolled Taquitos 3 for 1.35
Taquitos w/Guacamole 3 for 1.70
Taco Al Pastor 1.40
Fish Taco 1.70
Carnitas 1.75

ENCHILADAS

1 Cheese Enchilada 1.50
2 Cheese Enchiladas............. 2.90
1 Hamburger Enchilada........... 1.50
2 Hamburger Enchiladas 2.90
1 Chicken Enchilada 1.60
2 Chicken Enchiladas 3.10
1 Beef Enchilada 1.60
2 Beef Enchiladas 3.10

BURRITOS

Carne Asada Mix 2.59
Carne Asada Burrito 2.59
Beef 1.99
Hamburger 1.60
Chicken 1.99
Machaca 2.19
Bean 1.49
Chorizo 2.19
Mixed 2.19
Chimichanga 3.15
Fish Burrito 2.39
Carnitas 2.59
Chile Relleno 2.29
Burrito Al Pastor 2.29

TORTAS

Beef Torta 2.49
Chicken Torta 2.49
Carne Asada Torta 2.89
Carnitas 2.89

TOSTADAS

Bean Tostada 1.40
Hamburger Tostada.............. 1.55
Chicken Tostada................. 1.70
Beef Tostada.................... 1.70
Quesadilla 1.60
Chile Relleno 1.65
Tamale 1.20

BURGERS

Deluxe Burger................... 1.05
Cheese Burger.................. 1.30
Plain Burger .... .80

French Fries .... .75
Bunuelo........................ .75
Rice .... .80
Beans .... .80
Hot Carrots .... .60

EXTRAS

Sour Cream .... .45
Cheese .... .45
Guacamole .... .60

Ground Beef...$2.70

**FLYING
SAUCER
SHREDDED BEEF
$2.99**
Chicken $2.99

BEVERAGES
Med. .75 Lg. .85

Coke
Dr. Pepper
Sprite
Diet Coke
Milk
Iced Tea

Med. .85 Lg. .95

Horchata
Jamaica
Coffee   .50

BEER
Domestic
$1.50
Imported
$1.99

WINE
Chablis
Rose'
$1.25
a glass

TAX IS NOT INCLUDED

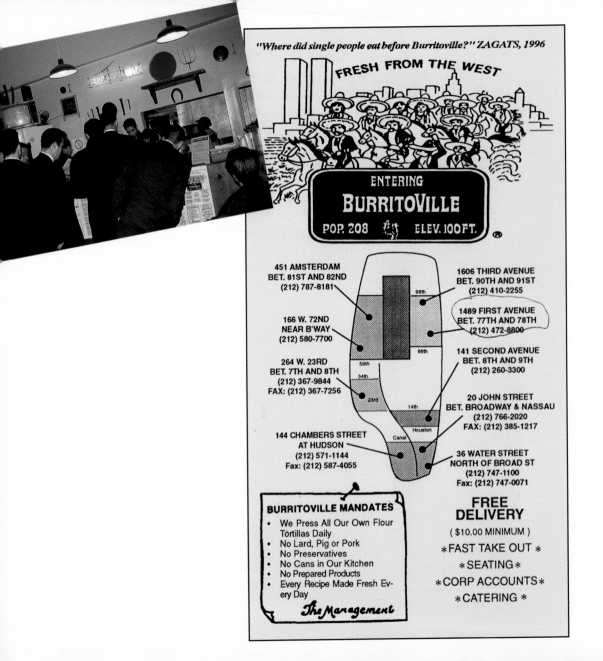

Burritoville

144 Chambers St., New York, New York, (212) 571-1144

The flagship location of one of New York's few successful taquerias (Burritoville has eight other sites in Manhattan) actually lives up to its "Fresh from the West" claim. The ingredients are top-notch, and the effort to produce a quality product is evident in the enthusiasm of the Spanish-speaking workers.

Burritoville serves sixteen different burritos, but the Mystical Frisco Burrito and the Fajita Burrita are the simplest and best offerings. At $5.50 and $6.25, respectively, these burritos are some of the cheapest available in Manhattan. All of the right elements are present, and although only black beans and brown rice are available, the burritos show excellent ingredient integration. The thick and hearty tortillas are made in the back room, helping to make this one of the most authentic burritos in New York. Burritoville's salsa is the hottest around, although the red kind can get a bit mushy. When asked if good burrito ingredients are hard to get on the East Coast, Burritoville workers respond in typical New York fashion, "Of course not—everything is available in this town."

Founders Steve Lynn and David La Point are rightfully proud of their creation and have been attracting a loyal following since opening their first restaurant in 1992. While they admit that many New Yorkers don't really understand taqueria culture, Burritoville's commitment to service, health, and freshness have solidified their popularity. Mr. La Point points out that "New Yorkers know what they want, and all we do is give it to them." According to the enthusiastic owners, the Ramones and the Beastie Boys rely on Burritoville deliveries to get them ready for big concerts.

The late 1990s have brought us a radically changed New York City. First, Times Square became a family attraction center, then the Jets won some football games, now one can get quality burritos in deepest Manhattan. Will wonders never cease?

Honorable Mention

While it may be an injustice to not give the following taquerias a full review, it would surely be a greater crime to omit them altogether.

Gallegos Brothers Mexican Deli
1424 Broadway, Santa Monica, California, (310) 395-0162

The outdoor patio is a perfect spot to enjoy the Southern California sun while eating a perfectly constructed and highly seasoned chicken burrito. The deli counter fronts a full-fledged corn tortilla factory that has been family-owned for over fifty years. Three generations of Gallegos family members keep

the business in operation and will be happy to explain the tortilla-making process or tell you stories about all the famous people who have dined in their restaurant.

Taqueria Pico de Gallo
2618 South 6th Ave., Tucson, Arizona (520) 623-8775

Though the burritos are not especially notable, the carne asada at this South Tucson hole-in-the-wall was so good, and the atmosphere so authentic, that we could not ignore it.

La Costena

2078 Old Middlefield Way, Mountain View, California, (650) 967-4969

Originally an unassuming burrito joint located in the back of a Mexican super-market, La Costena has become a rite of passage for Silicon Valley burrito lovers. The delicious burritos are assembled to order as you select your options from a dazzling array of fresh ingredients.

Caramba

5421 West Glendale Ave., Glendale, Arizona, (602) 934-8888

The burritos at Caramba do not contain beans or rice, but the meat is carefully prepared and the four types of salsa are superior. Don't be scared off by the fast-foodish architecture.

Baja Bud's

11819 Wilshire Blvd., Santa Monica, California, (310) 393-6060

It's a chain with clichéd southwestern decor, but Bud's is definitely committed to quality food. The burritos are well constructed and the chips are made fresh on-site. A taqueria for the Noah's Bagels crowd.

El Tarasco

316 Rosecranz Ave., Manhattan Beach, California, (310) 545-4241

El Tarasco is notable for its smooth integration of beach culture and taqueria culture. While it may be possible to find more authentic ingredients, it's the perfect spot after a long day at the beach. The cramped counter sits almost on top of the surf-sticker-plastered kitchen, and you may have to wait to sit down; but if you've got a big appetite and don't mind sloppy burritos, it's worth it.

Anna's Taqueria

1412 Beacon St., Brookline, Massachusetts, (617) 739-7300

The price is right, the music is Mexican, and all the correct burrito ingredients are present at this stylish, bright, and cheery little taqueria. The only drawback is that the burritos were not seasoned or spicy enough for our taste.

El Famous Burrito

7047 Clark St., Chicago, Illinois, (773) 465-0377

Located in the largely Latino Rogers Park area, El Famous dishes out huge burritos in fitting surroundings. The delicious burritos at El Famous are almost enough to make Chicago's numbing winters tolerable. Almost.

113

Hasta Luego

AHS-tah LWEH-goh

See you later . . .